{FROM CUBICLE
TO T
NEXT INTERNET }

FORWARD BY JOEL COMM

JAIME LUCHUCK

madeeasy
PUBLISHING
An Imprint of Morgan James Publishing
NEW YORK

FROM CUBICLE SLAVE TO THE NEXT INTERNET MILLIONAIRE

ISBN: 978-1-60037-372-5 Paperback

ISBN: 978-1-60037-371-8 Hardcover

Published by:

madeeasy
PUBLISHING
Made Easy Publishing
An Imprint of Morgan James Publishing
1225 Franklin Ave Ste 325
Garden City, NY 11530-1693
Toll Free 800-485-4943
www.MorganJamesPublishing.com

Cover Wrap Layout & Interior Design by:
Heather Kirk
www.GraphicsByHeather.com
Heather@GraphicsByHeather.com

Cover Wrap Concept & Design by:
Fletcher Groeneman

{ DEDICATION }

To my parents, Fisherman Cal and Shelley, my most devoted and proud cheerleaders; Ryan, Stacey, Travis… and everybody else supportive in my life (hey — you know if you belong in that category or not).

PS: I couldn't have done it without you and your unfaltering support.

IV

{ INDEX }

{ SECTION 4 } Competition Continues

{ SECTION 5 } Next Steps

{ SECTION 6 } Appendix

{ AN INITIAL FYI }

I was a contestant on the online reality show *The Next Internet Millionaire* (NIM). The show was the first of it's kind, as no one had ever attempted a competitive reality show exclusively for the web. It was the brainchild of Joel Comm, successful Internet marketer and author of the *New York Times* bestseller, *The Adsense Code*. The show was shot for an emotionally gruelling and obscenely hot two weeks in Colorado during the summer of 2007.

Before the show, I worked in the daily 9 to 5 grind. Winning the show did not make me an instant millionaire but it gave me the tools to become successful. It is these tools that I am sharing with you.

VIII

{ FOREWORD }
BY JOEL COMM

We live in very exciting times. The Internet is booming, and in doing so, opening doors for thousands upon thousands of people with a dream and a vision. In fact, I would be so bold as to say that there has never been so much opportunity afforded to so many as there is in this age of technology.

And yet even with so much opportunity, many people are afraid to take the leap into the unknown… to risk the status quo for the hopes of attaining their dreams. Nothing happens without taking action, and that's what this book is all about.

Jaime Luchuck was selected to be a contestant for "The Next Internet Millionaire" reality show because of her creative flair and willingness to take risks. She proved that she was prepared to leave her job and launch out into a new career as an Internet Entrepreneur.

I must confess that her musical audition captured my imagination the first time I saw it. And on the set of the show, she impressed me with her desire to give the competition everything she had and not quit though the odds appeared stacked against her.

From Cubicle Slave to the Next Internet Millionaire is one person's behind-the-scenes look at the world's first competitive Internet reality show. But even more so, it is the story of a young woman who was willing to say "enough!" to the rat race and pursue her dreams.

Not only is Jaime's recounting of the events entertaining and insightful, but she also shares valuable information she gleaned from some of the world's leading marketers who appeared on the program. From list building and branding to copywriting and viral marketing, this book is a resource that will help you build your business faster and smarter than ever before.

Are you ready to be like Jaime and take a leap forward into your dreams? You only go around once in this life, so it's important to take risks and seize opportunity. Its time to leave the cubicle and do something extraordinary... be the Next Internet Millionaire!

FINAL
{ JUDGEMENT }
ROOM

It's been a long two weeks. Insanely long and gruelling. In a way, I feel like I have been living this high stress, high tension, high emotion life for years.

Charles Trippy, the other lucky finalist, and I just gave our final presentations to the judges.

Oh my god — final presentations! Two weeks, and it comes down to here and now.

Outside of the Classroom set, I'm pacing. My hands slap against my thighs rhythmically as I walk back and forth in the warehouse, anxiously waiting for the crew to set up the JUDGEMENT ROOM.

The Judgement Room, the room where teams go and return a member or two short. The room teams go in anxious and fearful, and return emotionally beaten to a pulp, the ones staying secretly relieved that their team-mate went home and that they are around to fight another day.

This is the room that Charles and I are waiting to go into. Us two… the final two. But this time, when we go into that room, one of us will be eliminated, and one of us will become the Next Internet Millionaire.

Charles and I are very different but very similar, if that makes any sense (I've only known him for two weeks, so this is a broad analysis). He and I seem pretty capable of handling high-tension situations. And, we are both interested in film and video.

XI

But where we differ is that I need to be the Next Internet Millionaire and he doesn't. I mean, it would be nice for him, sure, but he doesn't *need* to win. He's already doing what he wants to do — he gets paid by You Tube to make videos for his many adoring fans. I work for the Ontario provincial government making/monitoring content management system websites. It's basically a glorified data entry job with a bigger and better title. Not fun. Not creative. Not at all inspiring. It's a union job too — but don't get me started on the "merits" of a union workplace. In my opinion, "Hey, I've been here longer," is not a legitimate reason to earn way more money than newer employees who do the same job or even know more than you but haven't "put in their time". What ever happened to hard work?

Strangely enough, even though I'm standing outside "the room", I'm not actually nervous. Every other day of the competition, I have been nervous. Worried that I'll be eliminated, that Joel Comm won't see in me what I know is there. That I'll let my family down. That I'll embarrass myself by being one of the first to go home. That I'll look out of my league.

I took time off from work to be here. Unpaid leave. All of my allotted vacation time FOR THE YEAR. And the show's producers decided that once we're eliminated, we can't go home and back to our lives. For me, that meant that if I was eliminated from the show, I would be wasting money and future vacation time putzing around in Colorado as well as not winning the competition. I had no interest in that.

You see, they had put a bunch of $$ into the show and no one was supposed to know the outcome before the show aired. By us going back to our lives, people would know approximately where we ended up placing. So, even if we didn't *tell people*, they would know.

"Quiet on set."

Soon... the moment of truth (cheesy, I know, but true).

I hug Charles. He is nervous — funny since he initially came to Colorado as a joke.

It could get nasty in the Judgement Room. Every other time I've gone in with people I'd become friends with, I left feeling friendless. Inside that room, the judges make each contestant pinpoint who they think should go home and why. It might make for good TV, but it leaves a lot of hurt feelings. Since we are down to the wire, they could likely make us plead our case of not only why we should be the Next Internet Millionaire, but why the other person shouldn't. And picking at other people's weaknesses is never a good thing for relationship building.

"Roll tape... Action!"

It's time.

We walk quietly but confidently into the room, the two of us in a straight line. The Judgement Room is strategically set up to intimidate. And it does this well. From the panel of judges lined up on one side of the table, facing the contestants... to the fact that they are all given full glasses of cold water and we have nothing. You know when you walk in that they are the bosses and you are at their mercy.

We sit down in the designated "contestants" leather chairs. My eyes are insanely sore and bloodshot from two weeks of staring into harsh, hot stage lights, my body very ready to be off camera.

Charles is nervously fidgeting, shifting constantly in his chair. I look over at him and smile reassuringly.

The judges walk in... Rich Schefren, Heather Vale and Joel Comm.

People, these are some big names.

XIII

Rich is called "The Coach to the Internet Gurus." Okay, I am not even an Internet marketer yet, let alone a guru. This guy turned a regular family clothing store in New York City into Soho's hottest eclectic clothing boutique. He invested in a hypnosis center that grew to generate over $7 million per year. Per year! And then he decided to create a product that has revolutionized business coaching, the Business Growth System. Hmmm, yeah, he and I are on the same level.

Heather is from Toronto, like me (Go Canada!). She has remained relatively distant to us contestants over the course of the competition. I doubt she is normally as cold, but instead, strategically decided to be in order to remain in a position of power. Heather does what I would love to do. She began her media career in 1993. She's been a host and a producer on television, and she has worked in Internet TV production, print and on the radio. Now Heather has created a real niche for herself, she's like the "Barbara Walters of the Internet". She interviews huge Internet marketers and tons of other successful people. Um, can I have her life?

Joel… well, Joel is who we, the contestants, really need to impress. He is the host of *The Next Internet Millionaire* — this is his thing. He invited me to be a contestant on his show based on two audition videos. I put together two silly two-minute videos (one about how much money I spend on coffee at Starbucks — seriously, it *is* a ridiculous amount; the other, a musical). I mean, they're fun, but I know nothing about Internet marketing. I have a lot to prove to this guy — and I'm sure he's seen a lot of talent. I mean, he's Joel Comm. The guy is the Adsense genius. He wrote a *New York Times* best-seller called *The Adsense Code* (the cover cleverly designed like *The Da Vinci Code* book cover). "But wait… there's more!" (an Internet marketer's catchphrase). Before the Adsense stuff, he created an online games company that Yahoo ended up buying. Now it's Yahoo! Games. Joel has been entirely unreadable this whole competition. He hasn't been hanging around with the contestants (well, he has invited some of them over to his house for a movie night... but not me, I didn't win the challenge that prize was awarded to).

So yes, the judges at that head table are a bit intimidating. I mean, don't get me wrong, I don't get intimidated by people. People are people are people — everybody goes to the bathroom. But there is a lot of success sitting at that table, and they are making huge life decisions for me.

Here's a concern. From about Day 4, many of the contestants have been dubbing Charles Trippy "Joel's Golden Boy", the "You Tube King", the "shoe-in". I've always tried to be secure in my potential (keep my confidence up) — but both of our presentations were good. Will Joel want to go with Charles? He might be more of a safe bet. He has that huge You Tube following, a list of something like 30,000 subscribers.

But I have qualities that Charles doesn't possess. I try to keep my mind focused on that.

It is dead quiet in the room... and hot, bloody hot. The judges sit staring at us. They all have good poker faces, I can't read any of them.

Joel begins his "final two" speech. He gives the "final whatever" speech every time a team is in the Judgement Room. Something serious about how we're down to *blank* number, he's gotta pick a joint venture (JV) partner. That person has to have blah blah blah qualities. Is there a person in front of him who has those qualities? He doesn't know...

Now it's time for the panel to question us about the merits of our presentations. From my past experiences in the room, the panel is usually pretty harsh. This time they were okay. The questions were valid, and the panel was not abusive. They started in

XV

on me first, each taking turns pointing out holes or problems and questioning my decisions. This time, though, they point out some good points too. Then they moved on to Charles and did the same song and dance with him.

Again, I have no idea which way the judges are leaning. Damn — I like to have at least an inkling!

Then I am asked to tell the judges why I think my proposal is a better JV idea then Charles' "How to make videos and money for You Tube" DVD series.

Hmmm — told you that was coming…

I don't even remember what I said — I just know I spoke. My mind was racing with all the potential benefits of my product. With the potential benefits to Joel of having me as his JV partner.

Charles speaks next.

Then they leave the room to deliberate. They leave us in the black curtained-off room, alone, with no water. Just theirs sitting on the table, the condensation forming little puddles on the black table.

By ourselves. Only Charles and me… and our anticipation of the end. And the judges' decision.

Thoughts like *What will I do if I don't win?* creep into my head. The past two weeks have been so crazy, so surreal, I haven't even had a chance to process what I've learned from the instructors. I haven't had any creative ideas (which is uncommon for me, so scary). What if I have to go back to my job? I really don't want to go back there — I hate it. But I push those thoughts out of my head… I have to keep thinking *I'm going to win; They're going to pick me; I deserve it.*

"Quiet on the set."

XVI

"Roll tape… Action!"

The judges walk back in, solemnly smug in the fact that they know our fates while we are clueless.

They slowly sit in their black leather chairs, and take sips of their waters. I take some pleasure in the knowledge that although they get water and we don't, that their water is no longer, in any way, shape, or form, nice and cold. The water glasses have been cooking under the hot lights for almost an hour now.

Charles shifts in his chair again. I sit perfectly still, anxiously awaiting their decision.

Then Joel speaks. He talks about the merits of my JV idea. He talks about the merits of Charles'. This is another of his dances, although usually in the Judgement Room, he talks about each contestant's flaws. So this is new. But it's still a back and forth dance before the final "voila!"

And I still have no clue where he's going!

Then he hits us with "I have some good news and some bad news for you."

Seriously, come on Joel, TELL US.

This has gone on long enough. Or has it been a long time? Maybe it just feels like it has been. I don't know. I have completely lost track of time since coming to the COMMplex. Hours, days, weeks, minutes, seconds — no idea anymore.

"The bad news is that neither of you will get the $25,000 prize."

What the %@#&?

"The good news is that I am going to do a JV with both of you!"

Pause. Pause. Pause.

What??

XVII

So we both win?

I am stunned. Shocked. I have been waiting for this moment for two weeks. Longer, actually. Since I first put in that coffee audition video, I have been waiting. Why do I feel nothing? It must be shock.

I'm not sure what to do, so I plaster a smile on my face, hug Charles and shake the judges' hands.

Whew — it's all done now! Time for the wrap party. Then time to go home.

Both of us doing a JV. That's a pretty cool twist. I doubt the show's audience will have guessed it. Granted, I'll admit, the $25,000 USD would have been a handy parting gift — I could have seriously used it. But the JV is — wow!

On my way out of the Judgement Room, Heather catches up to me to offer her congratulations. I'm sure she's glad that her fellow female Torontonian nabbed it. "Thanks" I say, still wide-eyed and dazed. She replies:

"NOW YOU CAN QUIT YOUR JOB!"

Huh?!

My mind blanks with panic. Quit my job? Well, yeah, that sounds great. In theory. I want to quit. Of course I want to… but, quit my job? Really quit my job? Seriously QUIT MY JOB??

Thousands of questions flash through my mind at warp speed.

If I quit my job — how will I pay my rent? How will I eat? How will I shop (hey — I'm a girl, what do you expect?)? Where will I live? What will I do?

It's not like I'm in love with my job, but quitting is another matter. I've worked hard to get where I am. Where is that, you might be asking? Well, right now I'm basically a web editor. Since

XVIII

it's a union job, I've been working my way up for quite some time now (well, that makes it sound like I've been in government for ages, It's actually been just under five years), but I don't have a union personality. Not at all. You can often find me at my desk working through lunch and in the office past five. I've been there long into the night on many occasions as well as on the weekends. I do not fit into the government box.

So, why am I scared to quit? I never thought the job I was doing would be permanent. Hell, they've never even bothered to make me permanent. I'm on contract. That means they keep me on my toes, always wondering (every three to five months) if I might have a job.

I've had co-workers who sleep on the job. I won't name them, but their habits, I believe, are well known — and they make more money than me… A LOT MORE. The "government mentality" drives me nuts.

And I don't really feel any loyalty to the place. My boss is a very nice woman but, in the past, she certainly hasn't hesitated to put my job on the line if someone more senior might need it. I do think she tries to be fair, though, and she has given me a lot of freedom. But still, she's like everybody else. People go to bat for themselves first. *So why*, again I ask myself, *am I scared to quit my job?*

Joel Comm wants to do a joint venture with me. That should mean mega bucks. And the knowledge I gained from being allowed to participate in his and Eric's show alone is phenomenal.

Eric Holmlund is Joel's business partner in this show. Together, *The Next Internet Millionaire* is their creation. Although he's not on camera, Eric is around for every decision. He's the one who is always shouting "Quiet on the set!" and "Roll tape… Action!" In business, Eric is known for being quite an excellent copy-writer.

And he began his marketing career on eBay years ago. And he's younger than me…,just.

But seriously, I get to partner up with these guys… I should be able to earn money for me from now on. Lots of it.

BUT I'M STILL SCARED TO LEAVE MY JOB.

I make $60,000 per year in my current job. Am I happy? No. Am I excited to go to my job every day? No. Do I take more sick days than I need to? Yes.

I have always known that I should work for myself, that I will some day work for myself — my biggest problem has been coming up with a plan. I have so many interests — but how does someone make money off of their interests? I didn't know.

In this book, I will show you how I went from being a cubicle slave to an entrepreneur. Sure I won *the Next Internet Millionaire* challenge, but you don't need that honour to get out of your situation.

I didn't win a million dollars. I learned from twelve Internet marketing geniuses. Twelve successful and very rich businessmen. They taught me business skills that work for every and any business, not just Internet marketing. They are twelve incredibly smart people who figured out how to live the dream, follow their passion. And they are very successful doing it.

These teachers, along with Joel and Eric, gave me the confidence to get out of the daily 9 to 5 grind, and now I want to help you get out too. There is nothing more discouraging than doing something you don't want to do. Why sit and daydream of you success? Why waste your time?

I want you to be happy. I want you to feel exactly what I feel. The elation, the freedom, the trembling fear of walking into your job and telling your boss… "I'm quitting, your loss," (a line from my musical audition video — more about that later) and the pride and sense of accomplishment you carry around after you do it.

So stop sitting around. It's time... "Quiet on the set!"

XXI

XXII

{ SECTION 1 }

9 TO 5

THE MYTH OF JOB
{ JOB SECURITY }

Wow — I can't believe how society is instilled with such a false sense of security from "permanent-nine-to-five-work-for-someone-else" work.

I wonder why that is?

What does permanent work offer us? Obviously, as people, we don't do something unless we get something out of it. So what could that something be? What's our reward for going into a job that we're not excited to do? Not proud to be a part of? That's not making us rich?

The main answer screaming out at me is: security. It's a nasty eight-letter word. And it's very paralyzing.

When we work for someone else, we receive steady, usually bi-weekly, paycheques. We can go to work, tired, bored... even drunk (not that I'm saying you should go into work drunk). And we still get paid!

We base our lives around that regular sum of money that gets automatically deposited into our bank accounts. Our lifestyles depend on it. How and where we live, what we eat, how we dress, where we dine, whether we drink bottled water from glass jars or tap water — it's all based on income — income that we earn from working at our steady job. Knowing what amount of money is coming in is a huge comfort. No stress, just "Yup, there it is," "Oh yeah, it's two weeks later, there it is," and again, and again, and again.

We also know that should something ever happen to our job, we have security. In Canada, we have UI (unemployment insurance). This can be collected bi-weekly and is a certain percentage of your previous income. We get this payout because while we work for our J.O.B.S. (Just Our Bloody Station in life), we pay into the fund. Entrepreneurs might look at this payout as a ridiculous waste of money, but job-ers love the security blanket.

Health insurance and benefits are another perk of having a job. Again, the safety net of knowing that if you get a cavity, your dentist visit should be covered by your insurance. If you get sick, your prescriptions should be covered. If you need to take long-term leave because of illness, you're covered.

All good benefits for sure, but what are the repercussions?

First off, the majority of people who work in their safe little nine-to-five jobs are unhappy. **Being miserable at your job causes undue stress to your mind and body.** Therefore, you get sick more often and have to use those safe little benefits more often. It makes you feel like you need them, that you'll be screwed without them. What a Catch-22.

Also, the majority of people want to take pride in their work, but working your butt off for joe-company doesn't make you feel proud. Working for anybody who tells you what you can and can't do isn't something that builds pride. Being proud of what I'm doing is so important for me. I love to get lost in projects — live, eat, and breathe what I'm doing. But I get so mad when I do that only to have the rug pulled out from under me later on. If you're your own boss, you can take pride in what you're doing, congratulate yourself on your success, and never beat yourself up just because you're having a bad day.

Make money for yourself. Why slave away to make a ton for somebody else while they pay you a measly salary? Even if the

4

salary they pay you is great (you know it's still measly in comparison to what you're making them) — if you're not happy, get out.

Figure out what you want to do, make a plan… AND GET OUT.

I know these are bold statements. But I'm going to share my knowledge with you on how I got myself out of my nine-to-five, work-for-somebody-else situation…how I GOT OUT.

{ ME ON A REALITY } SHOW?

I first heard about *The Next Internet Millionaire* reality show from my dad, Cal Luchuck. My dad is an amazing man. He grew in up Winnipeg, Manitoba, number three of seven children. His family didn't have very much money growing up. They lived in the North End, the "wrong side of the tracks". But that was ages ago. Now he's fifty-five years old, owns his own boutique advertising agency, and in the past year has started learning about Internet marketing. Not many people can use Photoshop, speak well enough to have other salesmen claim they could "sell ice to Eskimos" (to use an old Canadian saying), and change the oil in a car. Very multi-faceted. He and my mom, Shelley, got involved with Peaks Potential, a company focussed on growing and developing your millionaire mind. Then they tried StomperNet, a subscription-based Internet marketing training company, and finally, they joined Joel Comm's coaching club.

My mom is a great lady, but she's not a natural born entrepreneur. My mom's family is very Catholic and very diverse. She is the oldest of nine children. Some of them were born with the entrepreneurial bug. Others, like my mom, were not. But that doesn't mean she's not into self-development, though. At the age of fifty (she's now fifty-three), she went back to school and studied Production Accounting. She graduated this past spring and is now working for an oil and gas company in Calgary… and doing her website homework in the evenings.

7

I guess, before I go too much further, I should give you a brief introduction to me. If you watched *the Next Internet Millionaire* show, you might have a small clue. But you only got to see what the producers and editors decided to show you. And they only got to see what I decided to allow on camera. So, you don't really know me. Yet.

I'm the oldest of four children. My parents, whom you've already met, married young. They both grew up in Winnipeg, a city commonly known as Winter-peg for its extremely cold and vicious winters. Winnipeg is also a city black with mosquitoes in the summer months. My parents met while working at an A&W and got married only nine months after their first date — true love. And they're still together thirty-two years later — and still very much in love. They hug and kiss all the time and my dad rubs my mom's head every night when they watch TV.

They were young when they got married. My dad was barely twenty-three and my mom, twenty. Just before they had me, they moved to Regina, Saskatchewan (also known for frigid winters — what's up with that? Couldn't they have moved to Florida?). I was born at the end of November on Grey Cup Day. The Grey Cup is the Canadian Football League's Super Bowl. Fun for my dad, I'm sure, to have his wife in labor during the big game. Although I like to think I was worth it.

Anyway, to make a long story short (for now), my parents completed our family with Ryan, Stacey and Travis. There's eight years between me and Travis. My parents seem to have the formula down. We're girl, boy, girl, boy. And we're all exactly three years apart in school. Now that I think like an Internet marketer, I'm thinking they should write an eBook about that and sell it. They'd make millions!

Now, back to the auditions.

One day, I got a phone call from my dad (my parents live across the country from me in Calgary, Alberta — for you Americans, if you don't know, that's like New York City to Spokane). He had received an email from Joel Comm about the upcoming show. Being a member of the coaching club, he got regular emails from Joel.

He sounded so excited about it — he told me he was going to audition and he thought I should too. To audition, you had to create a two-minute video with only you in it, talking about why you should be on the show.

I grimaced. Seriously, I did. "I don't think so, Dad," was my reply.

He desperately wanted me to audition. I wasn't trying to be stubborn, I just didn't want to. Why? "Because I don't do reality TV." And that was true. I don't watch *American Idol*. I don't watch The Apprentice. I have never watched *Survivor* or *The Amazing Race*. I do have to admit, however, that I have watched an episode or two (or twelve) of *America's Next Top Model*. But still, usually, reality shows are ridiculous. They're about people trying to get famous. People who will do anything to get famous. And that's just not me.

Ever since I was a little girl, I always wanted to be an actress. I tried for a few years too. Did some independent movies. But I always said that I would turn down a role or a commercial that would make me look like an ass. And I stick by that… I would.

So, that said. I had no interest in Joel Comm's little reality TV show. None whatsoever.

But my dad was persistent. He kept asking me video production questions since he had never put together a video and he kept trying relentlessly to coerce me into putting one in too. "We can do a father/daughter thing, it'll be so great!"

No Dad!

Then he tried a different tactic. He told me he had decided he wasn't going to put in an audition — that he didn't have the confidence he would get anywhere with it. He didn't really know how to make a video and he was really too busy.

He sounded awful, dejected, and my heart broke. I could tell he really wanted this — for us to do this together. So I weighed my options... sure it was a reality show, but it was only on the Internet. Seriously, how many people would watch it? I was pretty sure the numbers would be minimal and, if I didn't tell anyone, I wouldn't be embarrassed in front of my friends.

And what were the chances that I'd really make it anyway? People from all around the world were submitting videos. Talented people. In that case, what would be the harm? Nobody sees the video, I make my dad happy, and I go on with life as I know it. Good stuff.

Plus, I really wanted to step outside of my comfort zone. I also took a Millionaire Mind Intensive course back in May through Peaks Potential and what they really focused on was changing mindsets. Basically they talked about the fact that what you are doing now, even though it feels comfortable, isn't really working for you, obviously, since you're not where you want to be. So, step outside of your comfort zone. Try something different. You'll get different results.

So I told my dad that I would put in an audition video if he did.

I wish you could have heard how happy he was. He was so excited — talking to me about his ideas, calling me every day for hours at a time. My boss didn't love that, I could tell.

He really wanted to push the father/daughter concept. I wasn't so sure. I told him I'd rather do my own thing, but said

10

that I'd mention his video in mine. That way, we'd drive traffic to each others' videos but it wouldn't be an all or nothing deal. It was all about popularity to get to the next round. They were judging the videos on other criteria too, but popularity was huge in this first round.

My dad decided to do a fishing-themed video (Internet marketing is like fishing, blah, blah, blah). It was cute, a little too darkly lit, but cute nonetheless. I was very proud of him for shooting it because he was nervous to get in front of the camera. He did take after take, by himself with a camcorder, trying to say what he wanted to say. And saying it the way he wanted to say it.

I shot a video confessing my addiction to lattes. I couldn't use any brand names in it, but I'll let the secret out now... I'M ADDICTED TO STARBUCKS GRANDE SOY LATTES ($4.73 CAN). Yes, Starbucks, I bow at your feet. I visit you daily. I give you all my money. PLEASE GIVE ME AN ENDORSEMENT DEAL.

Anyway, as I said, I'm totally addicted to lattes. I drink them daily and have for the past few years. I don't even want to think about what my total must be. They started off being my treat for going in to my J.O.B. And then they also became a little weekend treat. Yep, I'm a goner. I've even gone to two a day while writing this book.

Since I spend way too much on my addiction, I pleaded for Joel Comm's help. I mean, without exaggeration, I spend $33.11 per week, $146.63 per month and $1,726.45 PER YEAR ON COFFEE.

The video was cute, although cheaply shot on my little Sony camcorder. I edited it on my little Dell laptop (only 396M of RAM) with Premier Elements — so the process was painstakingly slow and unbelievably choppy to do without the right hardware.

11

But I wore my new coat. I pitched my dad's video at the end... I didn't really care.

But my dad did. He watched all of the other audition video submissions. He kept an eye blued to the NIM forum. He got people to vote for us. He called me daily, AT WORK, to report on our status and discuss our odds. My boss definitely did not like this. She did not know what we were talking about (she definitely wouldn't have liked that), she just knew I was on the phone. Dad even began planning and filming his second video (the producers were narrowing down the field to fifty and those fifty were expected/asked/encouraged to enter a second video).

I have to admit, I didn't even think about a second video. I was busy at work, busy going out with friends... and busy planning my summer vacations. Why would I bother doing something when it could possibly be a waste of my time?

The cut-off for first round votes was a Wednesday night at midnight. My dad and I spent Thursday constantly checking our email, making sure we didn't miss Joel Comm's email telling us that we made it into the top fifty. I got caught up in the excitement. I never thought I would — but I can't resist a good competition. Plus, I hate to lose. Ask anybody.

Thursday night around 8:00, I got my email. I called up my dad... "So did you get yours?" I was actually convinced that both he and I would get on. I had never even considered otherwise. I totally bought into that father/daughter gimmick. But no, he hadn't received an email. "Maybe it's coming," I consoled him. "They might be sending one at a time." But he never got an email.

The top fifty were posted the next day and Fisherman Cal Luchuck wasn't one of them. I felt really awful. This was his thing. He wanted it. He wanted us to do it together. I didn't want to do this alone. We were a father/daughter team. What happened to the team?

But he's an amazing dad. He was so proud. He was so excited for me and all the possibilities that could open up for me. He wrote me this long email gushing his pride, and telling me that he knew as soon as he heard about this competition that it was for me, that I could and would win it. He had so much belief in me and my abilities — it made me feel so special.

It also dumped a lot of pressure on my shoulders now that I was the only one of us to continue on. I had to give him something to live through vicariously.

And now it was time to create another video. Like I said, I hadn't put any thought into it beforehand, something about not counting chickens before they hatch, blah blah blah. And, of course, there was the fact that I hadn't been too interested. But now was the time. It was late Thursday night and I had to have this next video in to the NIM producers on Tuesday. That meant I had five days… and I was idealess.

I decided to sleep on it. Not that I'm at all a morning person (I get up about fifteen minutes before I leave my house, and I hit snooze around five times before I even get up), but I figured something would hit me. Ideas do tend to hit at the oddest moments.

The producers had said that a second video was optional, but for me there was never an option. I was convinced that their saying it was not required was a trick to weed out the people who were too lazy to bother and the people who didn't really care. For some people, it's enough to come up with one great idea. In my opinion, if you can only do that… why would Joel Comm want to do a joint venture with you? Plus, some people entered as a joke — doubtful they'd put in the effort of another joke video. I was certain that a second video was a must.

13

I still needed an idea.

I wanted something different… something wow.

Friday morning, on the subway train to work, it hit me… a musical!

I called up my dad and told him my idea. "That's a little ambitious, don't you think?" was his answer.

No, I don't. Go big or go home, right?

Next step was to call up my brother, Ryan. He's the musician in our family. He even taught himself to read using Beatles records. He plays guitar, bass guitar, piano, has his own band, The Ryan Luchuck Band, and sings. He also just recently taught himself sax and trumpet… just because. He does all that and doesn't even know how to read music.

I asked Ryan what he thought of the musical idea. "I think that's a bit too ambitious, Jaime. Why don't you think of something else?"

But I really liked my idea — and I knew I could do it.

The thing is, I knew I needed Ryan on board or I couldn't do it. He's my music guy. I can play "Heart and Soul" on the piano and that's about it for my music skills (i.e. they're very basic). Unfortunately for me, he had a recital going on that weekend and was teaching singing during the day. He also works weekend nights as the "piano man" at a bar. But I managed to convince him that we could do this project somehow. Gotta love the art of negotiation. I was so excited.

Wow — project management is a wonderful skill to have and I don't come naturally to it. The "boss" part, yes, but I am not an organized person in the least. My room was always messy as a kid. My mom even tried charging me a nickel per article of clothing she had to pick off my floor, that didn't help. She upped it to a quarter per piece — I paid that too (how I got this money, I don't remember). I probably racked up the debt and worked it off in chores. Regardless, as a grown-up, my apartment is kind of messy. And I can rarely pre-plan going to the grocery store so I often end up either ordering take-out or eating nachos for dinner. My sister, Stacey, she's the organized one. I'm going to make her a project manager one day.

But when I want something, I work to make it happen. And I do like to be the boss. I feel more in control. I love to delegate (to competent people). I told my mom that I was fine with a clean room; I had nothing against it, so if I had to pay her to keep it clean, so be it.

Anyway, now that Ryan was on board, I had to check with my regular camera guy, my amazing friend, Philip Sword. Philip and I met in acting class years ago. We were dedicated to becoming actors. However, as happens to most aspiring actors, neither of us is really still in the business. But that doesn't mean we don't like to work on creative projects. So I called him up, asked him what he thought of the idea and if he was available to shoot it (he also shot my coffee girl audition). He loved the musical concept and was on board.

That lunch hour I wrote the lyrics:

Today is the day

Today is my day

Today is the very best day

I must look my best

There's no doubt about it

I'm so very happy

I just want to shout it

'Cause I'm going to work

15

Going to talk to my boss

I've got four words to tell her

I'm quitting, your loss

It started with pennies

I put them in my jar

Then with knowledge from Joel Comm

I became an earning star

She's a girl from the prairies

Who moved to the East, to the big city

A girl full of ideas but lacking on outlet

Oh what a pity

"There goes Jaime, that girl's so smart"

"I'd JV with that girl"

"I voted you a ten, Jaime"

Now I'm done with that job

I can work just for me

Keep on learning from the expert

Be financially free

I can give back

To my family and friends

I can help them earn

Lots of dividends

So thank you for voting for me

Now I'm the Next Internet Millionaire

Yes thank you for voting me

It's great to be the Next Internet Mill-ion-aire!

That was quite a dream

So excited I could scream

So Joel put me on your team...

Watch out Colorado!

Okay — so I had lyrics that I liked. That step was done. That night, I looked through some Disney videos. I called my brother and left him a message of Beauty and the Beast's "Bonjour" song as an example of the kind of style I was looking for. His plan was to get home from work around 2:30 Saturday morning and then put something together. I was to leave the phone by my bed so I could pick up the call and give my opinion.

All went well. From what I remember mid-sleep, I liked what he had put together. I talked to him briefly in the morning and heard it again. Then, he emailed me an MP3 of the song so I had it handy for choreography.

Schedule-wise, I wasn't going to be able to get into his studio to record it until Sunday, the next day, because of his recital. I was going to have to shoot the video to his voice.

That afternoon, Philip came over and we planned out shots to the lyrics. We hunted down some good locations and I thought about wardrobe. I also had to tidy up my house a bit since we were doing some of the shooting inside.

Sunday afternoon, we shot the video. Sunday night, we went over to Ryan's to record the soundtrack.

Monday morning, Ryan emailed me the final MP3. After work, I downloaded the video from the camera and edited it (unbelievably frustrating on this Dell — can't even count the

17

number of times I swore). Trying to match picture with voice is so important with a musical, and it was virtually impossible. But I did the best I could with what I had to work with and was happy with the results.

Then I rendered out the video and sent it in to NIM.

Whew! Done.

The second round of audition videos was to be live for two weeks. During that time, people could vote for your video (1 to 10). The judges were marking the videos based on professionalism, communication skills, how good you would be for the show, your creativity and your popularity. I thought I stood a pretty good chance.

My dad watched all the second-round videos. Surprisingly, there were quite a few who didn't submit second videos. We wrote them off our guess-lists right away. And there were some who didn't follow the rules... like having other people in the video, or wearing branded clothing.

My dad was my devoted cheerleader. He sent emails around to all his colleagues asking them to vote. I had votes from all around the globe — very cool. He didn't want to miss any chances to help me get in.

The two weeks ended and now it was all about waiting. Waiting to find out whether I would be one of the lucky twelve selected to go to Loveland, Colorado to compete.

I religiously checked my email all day Thursday; my dad checked in with me. Nothing. I had started to care about this competition — started looking forward to the potential this held for me. And nothing from them...

I decided the wait would be easier with sour gummy worms (seriously, they help every situation)... so I zipped across the street to the grocery store.

I was right, gummy worms helped the tension. I checked my email… still no word. Maybe I didn't get in?

I had booked three weeks off work, just in case. The first to go to the cottage with family. My grandparents have a cottage at Star Lake in the Whiteshell National Park, about two hours from Winnipeg. The next two weeks were in case I got to go to Colorado. I mean, with a job, if you don't book the time way in advance, you don't get the time.

Checked the email again… nothing.

Later that night I picked up the phone to call my dad and realized that I had a message. I checked it and it was Eric asking me to call him back. **I did, A.S.A.P.** He asked me if I was available for those two weeks. Um, yes. He asked if I could keep a secret from everybody about it. Um, yes. Then, he told me I was one of the twelve finalists! Ah-ha!

I was going to Colorado!

AND I COULDN'T TELL ANYBODY.

Hmmm, how to deal with my dad. Luckily, they were planning to announce the contestants one by one and I would be the first girl announced. This announcement would be Wednesday.

It was only Thursday.

I told people the show delayed their decision until Wednesday — that shut them up. Thank God I wasn't the contestant being announced the day before we arrived in Colorado. I'd honestly be interested in knowing whether some of those contestants kept the secret. How could your spouse not know if you were flying out of town the very next day for possibly two weeks? Hmmm, maybe they talked to Eric about special circumstances. I don't know.

19

WORKING
{ 9 TO 5 }
NOT A WAY TO MAKE A LIVING

I didn't always work for the government. I have a lot of interests — and I tried to find ways to make money from them.

The very first thing my mom has written down in my early childhood book under Jaime's Careers is "cookbook maker." Yep, I guess that's what I wanted to be when I was four. Hey, it sounded like a cool job.

When I was growing up, I always changed my bedroom furniture around. Probably monthly, I'd find a way to rearrange everything, moving it all by myself (and I was not a very big person). It was always different. So then, I wanted to become an interior designer. That was the plan, at least, until my parents told me that interior designers didn't make very much money and that I should instead find a job that paid well, then design my own house. I was sold — that was the new plan. But how to actually make all that money?

When I was twelve I was cast in a television commercial and that sealed my love for acting. It was a local Ford dealership commercial and I was cast because they wanted to use my soap-box car (I raced for two years — and won a lot). They wanted my car for the ad and my dad said, "You can use the car, but then you're using my kids." Voila — my brother and I were in. So I didn't really earn that gig, but I did upgrade my part to a speaking role. I got to say, "Yeah, sure is." Very cool.

I basically grew up on camera. My dad got our first video camera when I was about one month old and it was on me from

21

that day on. I learned to walk on camera, talk on camera. I went to the potty on camera, had baths on camera. Sang and danced in front of the camera... seriously, is it any wonder I love acting in front of the camera? There is one video clip where I'm starting to cry (I think I'm one and a half), and my mom says "Oh, don't be sad for the camera." I learned quickly.

So I told my parents that I wanted to act. They responded with "Well, write a letter to the TV station and if they want you to act, they'll call you." And I did. I wrote my letter and sent in a photo (from the family album)... but no one ever called back. Of course, years later I discovered that is not at all the right way to find work as an actor and that my letter would have gone right into the trash-can. Oh well... that dream was put on hold. When I was older, my parents encouraged me to find a job that "made money" — and told me I could "act on the weekends." Yeah, more on that later.

I think I was one of the only kids in high school who had no idea what I wanted to do when I grew up. I thought about physiotherapy (since I have relatives in that field), I thought about law (since I have relatives in that field), but neither really interested me.

I thought about journalism, since I like writing, or business, since I thought one day I'd own my own (but in what I did not have a clue). Eventually, since I needed to pick something, I decided to pursue the journalism thing and signed up.

When you really don't know what you want to do and you're not passionate about what you're doing — you don't do well. I discovered that the hard way. I mean, I didn't do badly in university... I just really wasn't too interested in the basic prerequisites: Statistics, Psychology, Sociology, English...

In high school I skipped classes — most of Grade Twelve in fact. I'm not exaggerating or bragging, it's just a fact. But I got very good grades so the teachers didn't/couldn't do anything about it, except for once. My Grade Twelve English teacher got fed up with my absences and called my house. My dad answered the phone. At that time, both of my parents worked out of town so they were very busy and not around a lot. Plus, I had been having a lot of lower back problems after having just recently quit gymnastics and dancing. My dad yelled at the teacher "She has a bad back! Her mother and I both work a lot. We can't call in. If she's not in class, she's at home." He slammed down the phone. That teacher never called again. Woohoo! Thanks Dad.

However, this meant I never learned good study habits and came to university with the same bad ones that I coasted through high school with.

I got a bunch of Bs in my first year of university — that was a shock to me.

I took a year off and moved to Calgary — out on my own. I was eighteen and felt very grown up. I started working at Safeway (a grocery store) as a cashier — hitting the big time, I know. This was not a career, but a way to get some cash while I figured out exactly what the heck I was going to do with my life.

It never came to me.

So, the next year, after my family had also decided to move to Calgary, and I moved back in with them… I went back to university. This time I went into Business.

That run didn't last long unfortunately, because I became very sick and had to drop out (more on this later).

It took me about three years to fully recuperate from my illness. Yes, it was very severe.

During that time, my dad left his job to start his own business. He opened up an advertising company, Cre84u Millennium Graphics, Inc. They did cash register till-tape advertising, and he

23

needed a graphic designer. So, who are you going to call? Not Ghostbusters, but your sickly, ghostly daughter.

I sat in the home office, a skinny, pale girl wrapped in a blanket in front of the new Mac computer, and I learned everything about Photoshop by trial and error. I had never really used a computer before other than to type up reports in school, and maybe using Print Shop to make greeting cards when I was in Grade Six.

Graphic design was a new thing for me and I loved it! I loved figuring out new ways to do things. Ways to make ads jump out. Ways to catch the eye of the customer. Ways to make them better than anyone had ever seen before. It was amazing. I looked at everything in the world in a new way. What font were they using? How did they lay that out? What benefit did they get by putting those colors together? How would I do it better?

I became extremely proficient with Photoshop. I trained my dad. I trained my cousin who also came on as a graphic designer. I trained my brother.

I was lucky enough to make ads for huge companies. I worked with McDonald's, Dairy Queen, Blockbuster, Walt Disney Co, Pizza Hut. It was so much fun. But I wanted to do more.

So, I went part-time with the company when I started feeling a bit better, and got my diploma (with Honours) in graphic design and multimedia. In school, I learned about animation software, Flash (a web animation tool), HTML (a web language) and Premier (a video editing software). We didn't spend much time on each of these programs, but I now knew what could be done. I could see more potential in projects.

I immediately talked to my dad about opening a web department of the company. He agreed. I talked him into giving me a raise too. I made a whole $18 per hour while I worked on the web stuff (still $14 per hour for the graphic stuff). Not the best money,

I know, but hey, I was in my early twenties and working for my dad. What could I expect?

The web stuff was fun. I hired one of my friends from school and together we built a website for Cre84u. It was a hugely complex Flash site full of animation. It would never be used today, but the style back then was "show what you know". So we did.

I learned to pitch and sell. I was so nervous calling on clients with my spiel in hand. It was cold-calling too, which really sucked. I decided right then and there that I hated cold-calling and that when I had a business, people would come to me. That would be my definition of success.

I got a couple of clients and built them sites. Got them listed on Google. But, at that time, most companies didn't really have websites. My Calgary clients weren't too keen on being pioneers. Plus, my heart craved the big city... so I packed up my brand new Volkswagon Golf Wolfsburg and drove to Toronto with my ginger-coloured cat, Kahlua, on my lap. Yes, I really did. It took me... seven hours to Saskatoon where I visited a childhood friend, three to Regina where I visited another friend, six to Winnipeg where I visited relatives... then twenty-four hours to Toronto. What an insane drive... single lane highways, winding roads, cottage country traffic, construction. But I made it.

In Toronto, I cold-called large advertising agencies to see if they were interested in hiring me. I had my portfolio loaded with all the work I'd done in Calgary and at school. It was good stuff. I still use some of that stuff in my portfolio. But Toronto was snob-bish; they're/we're known for that.

Toronto totally idolizes New York. If I had come from New York with that same portfolio, I would have been hired. Since I was coming from Calgary, I was told "this stuff is amazing... come back when you have *Toronto experience.*" Seriously.

Eventually I left the agency-looking and entered the fashion world. I love fashion and shopping and thought it would be really cool to work at a fashion magazine. I talked to Canada's largest fashion magazine, *FLARE*, our *Vogue*.

Lucky for me, they liked my stuff and me and *hired* me on as an intern. I italicize the word "hire" because they didn't pay me anything. No money… but I was expected to look like I fit in at the magazine. It was totally The Devil Wears Prada. In fact, four years ago I wrote a screenplay about an intern at a fashion magazine who becomes a super-hero to give herself self-worth. I still have it if any producers are reading this — and it's really good.

Yes, the magazine was that bad.

Editors who didn't talk to interns. Interns with nothing to do. And I don't do well if someone is wasting my time. They didn't teach me anything, which is unfortunate since that is why I was there. I was also really beginning to feel like there was more to life than the latest lipstick. There were days when I just sat at my desk doing nothing (and no, I wasn't practising for government). But jobs were scarce and editors were loath to train people just so they could take over their jobs. There were six interns at *FLARE* while I worked there. What a great gig for a company — get people to work for you for free.

After a few months of working in the Art department and doing nothing but basic image dropping into the sample layout, photocopying and filing, I moved over into the Style department.

I got to be a bit more involved there. I even got to do some blurb writing, but my name was never published.

The Editor-in-Chief was Queen Bee — and she never acknowledged me. Not even once. I made cookies one Christmas and brought them in. She ate one, loved it, but when she found out an intern made it, she walked away without saying anything. I even saw her out at a trendy restaurant one night... nothing. Very nice.

So, after six months with FLARE, I left, this time going back to my original love of acting.

I took up temp work, so that I would get paid, but still have time to pursue acting. This time, I learned the proper channels.

The temp job I landed was working in the provincial government at the Ontario Rental Housing Tribunal. There, I entered landlord/tenant applications on people who hadn't paid their rent and I scheduled their hearings. It was totally brainless work and I loved it. Most of the people were nice and I didn't carry any of the work home with me. I just went to work, whipped through it, had plenty of time to do my own stuff (as we weren't always super busy), and I could take any time off for acting gigs. They even paid me $18.59 per hour, which was more than I made as a web designer in Calgary. What a great temp job!

Acting-wise, I was busy learning about the business. Acting is great, but if you're not a strong businessperson, you're not going to get anywhere unless you're one of the lucky few. You have to learn how to market yourself to a market that really isn't looking for you. It's a tough field and you really have to love it to pursue it. In fact, if you don't love it, don't bother.

They, the industry and agents, want you to be beautiful and thin...but if you are, too bad, they already have tons of girls who are beautiful and thin. If you're not beautiful and thin... well, get beautiful and thin... those are the girls who get work. Be different but be the same. Is anyone else bewildered here?

I landed an agent, which is very hard to do, and kept him for a while, but eventually went out on my own and looked for independent work. I had some success. I landed some auditions for student films. These are short films and are not usually very professional. They tend to not be too much fun because, as my acting teacher once told me, "the actor tends to be way more experienced that anyone else on set." That is never good. It makes for long arduous shoots with so-so results.

I landed other indie films too. It's a frustrating business because many films that you take unpaid time off work to shoot, never even get finished. And the producers owe you nothing. They don't even pay you in the first place… and if they don't finish it — too bad for you.

Anyone with a camcorder can be an "indie producer" so you really have to be careful. I landed the lead in a horror film. I was excited. Then, suddenly, after a delay in production, the film's opening sequence was rewritten to include graphic nude sex scenes with both male and female partners. No thank you!

Yes, lots of lesbian films. Nudity films. And, seriously, there's nothing wrong with a little skin. But if my dad and grandpa are going to watch the movie, it had better be tasteful and minimal. Besides, I think it's sexier to allude rather than to graphically show everything. We all know what happens in the bedroom and what people look like without their clothes on.

My largest role to date was in the movie Heartland Son. It's a feature-length movie that was shot just outside of Hamilton, Ontario. I play the female lead — a married woman who is having an affair with the lead character. It's G-rated so nothing nasty there, but it was fun to shoot and I worked with a great group of people. The film went to a few festivals, but never really got anywhere, though you can buy it on Amazon.com. That's show-biz, I guess.

Meanwhile, I was getting very frustrated with the whole business of acting. I hated the fact that I wasn't in control of my destiny. That someone else could say "no" to me by not even opening up the envelope that included my headshot and resume. (I even began spending way more money to buy clear envelopes, but to no avail.) I hated that they had the choice of looking through hundreds of smiling headshots to maybe pick me. Cold-calling again. Screw that — they don't get to have all that power. That didn't seem fair.

So I started writing my own screenplays. And, as it turned out, I had a knack for churning them out. I wrote my first one in two weeks. It got a lot of great comments from other actors, but getting industry people to read it was another story. Not easy. It sat.

I wrote another. And another. And another. And another.

I had written a total of five feature-length screenplays... AND THEY WERE SITTING IN A FILE ON MY COMPUTER.

I was enjoying the writing part way more than the selling so I just wasn't bothering to try. I realized pretty quickly that this wasn't the brightest idea so I decided I better get off my butt and try to sell some.

I opened a production company called Lunon Films (Lunon is a mixture of **Luchuck** and **Grenon**, my mom's maiden name). I still really like that name.

I made a cool-looking website and put together a team of people to shoot a trailer for a feature I wrote called Anonymous. It's the fashion magazine intern superhero movie. Log line: Every comic book legend starts somewhere. Don't steal that by the way... I'll sue you.

I had so much fun making that film.

I had planned to market that trailer to catch a production company's eye so that they would want to make the feature. You can check it out at www.JaimeLuchuck.com.

Unfortunately/fortunately, I had just finished writing a feature I was really proud of… my best one yet. I called it Underneath It All. I can't tell you the log line or I'd have to kill you. But know that it was very "of the moment" and unique. This one I was going to sell.

I thought about who would be great for it. I then put together a great package using my graphic design and advertising skills, made my cold call, then sent it off.

My first thought had been Sarah Polley. She is a Canadian actress who has also done numerous US films, including Go and Dawn Of The Dead. But, she likes Canada and wants to remain involved in the Canadian film industry. She had directed a short which was acclaimed, but had never shot a feature. She was perfect. Using her would also mean that I would still maintain some control but we could use her name and contacts. I loved it.

I called her Canadian agent and, unlike when I was an actor and tried the same agency, actually got through. This was a forward step… I was in the door. I met with the agent and gave her my pitch again and the package with the script. She read it, said it was really good, but that Sarah was working on her own feature right now. Damn! But she wasn't lying. Sarah's first feature as a director, Away From Her, came out last year.

Okay… next.

I thought about Hollywood. I was a bit nervous because of my experience with the Canadian film industry, but I had heard Hollywood was a little less full of itself and more welcoming. It should be noted here that a Canadian production company had offered to read my first script after I finished it, but put me off for over a year afterwards: "Sorry, haven't had time to get to it yet." Blah, blah, blah… just say "No thank you — we don't want to read it," and let me get on with business. And this girl was a friend of my aunt's. I couldn't believe it.

Anyway, I thought next of Flower Films... Drew Barrymore's production company. I called and left a message pitching my log line and that I was looking for a sister company to produce an amazing film with, a film that I thought Drew would be interested in being a part of. I honestly thought I'd never hear back. I went out about half an hour later to buy a slurpee and, when I was out, I got a call on my cell.

It was Flower Films calling to talk about my film!

I was floored, I mean, honestly floored. I mean, literally floored. I dropped down to the floor where I was hoping it would be most quiet so I could sound at least a bit professional. I was also floored since in Canada, if you're a "nobody", no film person will ever call you back. Ever.

But she (not Drew herself, someone who worked at Flower Films) did, and she was lovely. We chatted about the project. She seemed really interested. She asked if I was thinking about Drew for the lead... I said I was and that she'd be great for it. I was thinking more of Drew for the lead's friend, but hey, this is sales. Then she asked if it was a comedy. It isn't — it's a drama. She said that the company had been recently bought out by Warner Bros. and that they can only produce comedies. Now that sucked! But she asked that I keep Drew in mind for the lead... and wished me luck.

It was the best rejection I ever had... and it gave me the confidence to press forward.

I next thought of Reese Witherspoon. She's an actress around the right age, she has her own production company, and she seems to take risks with her projects (or at least she used to when she was younger). I called up her agent to find out how to get in touch with her production company. Then I called them and pitched the script. They asked to have it sent down so they could read it. Again, I thought, "This is great. Hollywood, so much nicer than Canada."

The girl read the script, liked it, but turned it down saying "Reese wouldn't play someone who'd had plastic surgery." Okay — I guess she's not as much of a risk-taker as I'd thought. Instead, she was doing cheesy movies like Just Like Heaven and getting blah reviews. Next.

I tried Charlize Theron and Naomi Watts, but got stopped at their agents' front doors. Too popular, I guess. And neither were really producers at that time. Although it might be time to give Charlize another call.

Then I got a nugget in Canada. My uncle knew a woman in the Canadian film industry. He thought maybe I should talk to her, get her advice. It's all about who you know… no?

I called her up. We'll call her Flake (because that's what she turned out to be). I talked to her about my plans for my film and asked my questions about the industry. Then, surprisingly, she asked me about my project. I told her. Then she asked to read it so, again, I shipped it off.

She loved it and wanted to produce it. She was going to sign me to a hip-pocket agreement for a year while she put it all into play. She drew up the papers and sent them off to me. I had a lawyer look at them, made a couple of suggestions, she updated them, I signed them, then I sent them off to her.

Then nothing.

I called…. Nothing.

I called again… was she blowing me off?

Yes she was. I got the news… she changed her mind. She didn't have time for the project. Still loves the idea, but can't do it right now. Great. Lovely. I'd wasted the past four months on

Flake. I guess it's good she backed out though if she wasn't going to bother with it. Then it would have sat for another year.

The next practical step, I decided, was looking for a writing agent. They can get you in the front door of large production companies who won't even look at unrepresented individuals. But writing agents are extremely, extremely hard to get. I sent off to one of the best agencies in Canada. And finally, after a long song and dance, he read my script and called.

HE WANTED TO REPRESENT THE SCRIPT.

Perfect. Perfect. Now I was in, I was sure. He signed me for a year. He was going to sell the script. He believed in it. Loved it.

That was a year and a half ago. No sale.

In the meantime, I was fed up with my rental housing job. I was calling in sick a lot — the old "hate my job and now it's making me sick" syndrome. My boss recognized that and knew they needed someone over at head office so he sent me.

I interviewed for that job — Administrative Assistant in the Assistant Deputy Minister's office. The title was too long, but I got the job and a raise. And I could now walk to work. All was good. But I worked with a miserable woman. She was convinced that I was trying to steal her job. I thought this was insanely funny. Why would I want her job — she was barely higher up than me. Oh well.

I stayed there about two months, then got a promotion to Administrative Assistant to the Legal Director. I was there about a month before the manager in Corporate and Electronic Communications called me up and offered me a contract working on the web in the Communications Branch. When I was admin staff, I was so bored that I kept doing extra work with graphic design, etc, so I guess I caught the attention of management. It's all about who you know, right?

Anyway, that's how I got to where I am. I've developed my position so much further than when I inherited it two years ago. I now do podcasts and online video. I've done Flash animation and a bunch of writing. It's really not a bad job… I just don't want it.

I don't like showing up for work at 9 (oh alright, 9:10). I don't like that people aren't dedicated to the job. I don't like that I have no interest in Municipal Affairs and Housing (the ministry I work for). I don't like that they don't pay me a private sector-type salary. I don't like that I have a colleague that takes naps at work. I don't like that when I have nothing to do, I have to sit at my desk and pretend. I don't like that I get scolded for being on the phone. I don't like that I can only take three weeks of vacation per year. I don't like that I often sit in useless meetings. I don't like that I have to be nice to people I don't respect……

I can go on and on and on.

Wait a minute — why am I scared to leave my job?

{ SECTION 2 }

WELCOME TO LOVELAND,
COLORADO

{ COLORADO }
THE BEGINNING

I had had no sleep. None at all. As I mentioned, my grandparents (my mom's parents) have a lakefront cottage at Star Lake (by the Manitoba/Ontario border). I've gone there almost every summer since I was a kid. I met up with my family there for a week before heading down to Colorado (week one of my three-week vacation).

I am British–Ukrainian. I will never get a tan on my white, white, whiter-than-white skin, but I love the sun. I slather on my forty-five SPF and enthusiastically head outside everyday and bake. Then reapply and bake — and repeat. I love sun, water sports, and everything cottage or beach.

So I was there for a week to enjoy the fun, the sun, and my father's NIM theories. Then I flew back to Toronto, getting to my apartment at 11:15 at night. My flight to Colorado was scheduled to depart just after eight in the morning the next day. I was going to have to catch the subway train at 5:55.

Of course a friend of mine from New York was flying in that night — and I rarely get to see the guy. It was only polite to make the effort to go out. So I showered away the cottage grime and one-eightied into club clothes. I got to the club, had a couple of drinks, visited, took a cab back to my place, unpacked from the lake, and began packing for Colorado. I had no idea what to bring since I had no idea what to expect.

Needless to say, I packed a very big suitcase. Work clothes, bum-around clothes, workout clothes, a swimsuit, it was all in my crappy Air Canada suitcase. I call it "crappy" because it got banged up and broken the second time I used it; the hard plastic inside is cracked, broken, and crumbling.

Then my cat got sick. Not nice. I spent the next hour and a half worried, on the phone to the vet, talking with my house-sitter, and cleaning vomit and poo off the carpet. There went my sleep time. And I was really worried — I thought about cancelling the trip because he never gets sick. I mean, I'm not a crazy cat lady or anything, but there was blood in his poo. That's never good.

But I went to the airport — leaving my house-sitter very strict instructions.

After a two and a half hour delay in St. Louis, I finally got into Denver. Tired — oh so tired. But excited.

When I exited into the reception area I heard my name being shouted...contestants Thor Schrock, Steve Schuitt, Alisande Chan, Christine Schaap, and Kaitlyn Stover (Eric's sister in-law and a really great person) were waiting for me. They recognized me from my videos and vice versa. It was so comforting to have them there. And I guess, because we all did videos, it was almost like being met by friends because I'd seen bits of their personalities in their videos and knew what they looked like. I felt really welcomed.

The NIM producers put us up in a really nice hotel, the Residence Inn Marriott. And, other than having a gold shirt of mine go missing from my bedroom closet, I had a really great experience there.

Each contestant got their own suite that first night. It was a pretty huge suite — it might have been bigger than my apartment. Seriously, I'm not joking. That fact might be sad, but it's true. The producers had left us each a really big welcome basket

38

filled with treats, a signed copy of Joel's *The Adsense Code*, a DVD called "Your Own Internet Business — Start Today!", and a Loveland, Colorado rock with my name on it. Unfortunately, I would end up having to leave mine at the airport on the way home since my luggage was way overweight. So sad.

I felt really spoiled, really respected, really excited… and totally exhausted.

A bunch of us went out for dinner that night but I really just wanted to go to bed. Since I'm an extrovert, I fought it as long as I could. I even went back to Alisande's room where she tried to explain poker to me, Charles and Christine. Thor already knew how to play. I was just too tired to concentrate, so, as much as I enjoyed the company, I excused myself and went to bed.

The next morning I got up in time to meet everyone for lunch. I think I felt even more tired. You know that feeling when you're so depleted that when you finally get some sleep, your body says "Hey, wait, I need more!" Yeah, that's how I felt.

Not fun, but I guess I deserved it.

Everybody was at lunch. The day before I'd met Jason Henderson, Charles, Alisande, Thor, Christine and Steve. Today I met Debbie Ducic, Jason Marshall, Laura Martin, Carly Taylor, and Nico Pisani.

I certainly had first impressions of people… but I didn't write this book to dish dirt, bad-mouth or hurt people's feelings. What I will say is that one major life lesson I learned throughout the course of this competition is that you should never go only by first impressions.

LIFE LESSON 1: Never judge people solely by first impressions.

People aren't always as they appear.

We all change given different situations. Some people show that they are truly genuine, others that they are conniving. Some like to gossip about other people. Some people crack under pressure—snap. Some people become true friends. Some people show themselves to be annoyingly analytical. Some people show they really don't care. Some are overly egotistical.

What I learned is that whatever my first impressions are — they are first impressions only and I should not let them cloud my future judgements. This is an amazing life lesson. I made friends with people who, given my first impressions of them, I would never have been friends with. Opposite feelings came out towards some of those I initially thought well of.

At lunch, we were all introduced to Eric. He told us all about the rules of the show. Not what was going to happen on the show (not at all), more about things like "don't talk to the camera people," and "pretend the camera's not there," or "there are no hidden cameras in your bedrooms." Stuff like that. They were very good, maybe too good, about not giving away anything about what was going to happen to us on the show or what we would be doing.

We had to sign NDA's (non-disclosure agreements). These, I believe, would come back to haunt some people. The basics of the agreement were that we were not allowed to talk to anybody about the happenings of the show — or really about anybody on the show. It had been decided that we would all stay in Colorado the entire two weeks so nobody would know where we ended up based on our homecomings. That meant that regardless of whether we were on or off the show, we couldn't talk about what we were doing. Anything could give something away.

This again proved to be another lesson about people. People entirely willing to sign agreements can flip on a dime anytime afterwards. Everybody signed these agreements, each of us knowing that if we did not sign, we would not be on the show. The alternates would be called. But it was still our decision to sign. It's amazing to me how many people have thus far either broken the agreement or are extremely unhappy with it.

Before bed, a few of us "networked" by drinking Costa Rican rum (courtesy of Nico) in the hot tub. Hey — it's totally business. And non-9-to-5 business is fun.

I tried to be smart and go to bed early. I even got to bed at a reasonable time (probably around midnight or shortly after), but I couldn't sleep. I barely slept at all. All the excitement — it was just like Christmas Eve.

COLORADO — THE BEGINNING

{ MARK JOYNER }
DAY 1 AND

W e were up early today, the group of us heading out together for breakfast before starting our big day. I'm not a breakfast eater, so I would have preferred to sleep in. I, very wisely and surprisingly organized, ironed my clothes the night before so I could just slip them on. Usually, in the mornings, I pick out my clothes two minutes before I step out the door — and forgo the iron. For Day 1, I picked out a nice pair of cream pants, a long black cap-sleeve top and a thick golden weave belt. Since I didn't know how long I would last on the show, it was critical to look as good as possible.

Laura and Carly had gone out for a cigarette (they were the only smoking contestants). When they came back, they told me that the camera crew were out in the lobby, waiting. We decided to walk out there in true Diva form, with our sunglasses on indoors. This was really the first day of cameras and we were not at all used to or comfortable with them. If they wanted to film, we were going to give them something to film.

Once the entire group arrived, we headed out into a gorgeous limo. The show went all out for us. I had never been in a limo that big before. Since there were twelve of us and a cameraman (later to be named Ben) inside, it was crammed full. We all received gift bags with goodies (I'm still not sure why we got body lotion), and ten e-COMMerce chips. And Joel-mail (ha — Top Model joke). Actually, just a note telling us a bit about the value of the e-COMMerce chips.

43

It was funny, when my sister found out I was going to be on a reality show, she laughed. When I asked what was so funny, she said she was picturing a Top Model experience in her mind. There, the twelve girls stay in a house with huge pictures of Tyra Banks plastered all over it. I had to laugh at that one, doubting that our home base would be covered with pictures of Joel Comm, but laughing at the hilarity of even the thought of it. How disconcerting.

The limo drove around for ages. I don't know Colorado; it seems like a relatively spread out state, we could have been going anywhere. Little did I know, we were basically driving in circles so the camera guy could get lots of footage (and probably so the show could capitalize on their limo rental — they used it that morning only).

The breakfast joint, McCoy's, had really good food. The poor waitress seemed a bit freaked out by the camera crew, but all went well. I ordered an omelette which tasted incredible, it's just unfortunate that it was wasted on me. I'm a Starbucks-for-breakfast kind of girl, so the omelette proved quite heavy. I also have a number of food sensitivities — dairy being one of them. It actually used to be an allergy for me. Whenever I ate it, my throat would close up and I would have a lot of problems getting air into my lungs. I was born with the allergy but the doctor's advice to my parents was "If it's not killing her, just keep giving it to her — the allergy will go away." And it did, although that doctor caused me a bunch of problems nineteen years down the road. When I got sick — I know I brought it up earlier and I will expand on it later, dairy, it was discovered, was one of the causes. Anyway, for about nine years I was off dairy completely. Then I decided, in a moment of pure unhappiness, to try it again, and I was okay (breathing-wise). So, I do eat it now, the allergy/sensitivity just exposes itself in another way (usually tiredness, blemishes, headaches, fogginess — you know, no big deal stuff).

So the omelette-for-breakfast thing maybe wasn't the best choice, but I don't always make the smartest decisions food-wise. I get tempted so easily by all the yummy stuff out there.

The breakfast gave me a headache and exaggerated my tiredness. I was not at my best. I really should have ordered fruit like Laura did. The only benefit from my heavy breakfast was that I/we (the contestants) were really not given a lot of opportunities to eat during the rest of the day so those breakfast calories had to last.

LIFE LESSON 2: Eat foods that encourage intellectual sharpness – not hurt it.

We arrived at the COMMplex, and had a chuckle at its name. By the end of the two weeks, many people vowed they would never use the word "complex" again. Ever.

Hmmm — I wonder if Comm is Joel Comm's real last name. Maybe he's really Joel Kosinski or Joel Brown and he decided to really capitalize on the whole dot com thing. I mean, really, how better than to change your last name? Comments, Joel?

Immediately upon entering the COMMplex, we were ushered into a room surrounded by black curtains. Twelve empty chairs awaited us. There was a stage with two large screens displayed. We all sat down. You could feel the excitement and nervousness pulsating through the room.

Heather came on the stage. Heather, from what I understand, talked herself into the job of co-host because of the abundance of testosterone on this show. The twelve gurus are male, and then there's Joel and Eric — she was right, let's get some women in here. I'm sure my fellow contestant Debbie Ducic ("Do you see? I see" — sorry, had to throw that one in) would agree.

Debbie is a huge advocate for women. She is involved with Gutzy Women, a company that supports the growth of women in business. Debbie, at fifty-three, was the oldest contestant but I was impressed with her entrepreneurial spirit. She is extremely focused on her Gutzy Women market and she champions them with everything she has.

I have to admit, though, I did start a Gutzy Women drinking game. I think Laura started one too so mine's not the only one out there. Debbie does mention "Gutzy Women" *a lot* so the game is whenever Debbie says either that or "Do You See? I See," you have to take a shot. Drunk fast, is all I have to say about that game. Sorry Debbie — I just couldn't resist. It's not a shot (ha! pun), plus look at how many times I plugged your company. I'd be drunk right now if I were playing my own game.

Heather welcomed us and introduced a video. We all sat back and watched. The video was of Joel, also welcoming us. Are you kidding me? He didn't even bother to show up?

But he did. He made his entrance after the video to our loud applause. Joel looks like he does in his videos, which might sound weird to say, since that should be obvious. But some people really don't look like they do on camera — they're not camera-genic.

Immediately the competition was on. Cresta Pillsbury of Hacker Safe was introduced.

Hacker Safe is a product that does what it sounds like it does, it protects websites from hackers. Consumers trust the Hacker Safe certification seal, and when it's on your website, your customers know that their information won't get out. Over seventy-five thousand websites use Hacker Safe. In fact, over half of the Internet **Top 500** (as reported in Internet Retailer Magazine) use Hacker Safe. Companies like Yahoo! use it — so it's definitely trustworthy.

Cresta, who was, as it turns out, my dad's customer service rep when he inquired about Hacker Safe (small world), and Joel announced that we were going to do a Hacker Safe Immunity Challenge. The person who won this challenge would be safe from elimination today. These kinds of Hacker Safe Immunity Challenges would continue throughout most of the competition. You can imagine, as our numbers dwindled, there was extreme value in winning that shirt (we were awarded a shirt that we would wear for that day and it would keep us safe from Joel, the dream hacker).

But today, we all really wanted to win this — nobody wanted to be eliminated on the very first day.

Our challenge was to stand up and present another contestant as the Next Internet Millionaire. We would have one minute to present and the judges, Joel and Cresta, would pair us up.

As soon as I heard we were going to public speak, my blood ran cold. I was coated in nervousness. My brain shut off.

Public speaking is most people's number one fear — and it is an excellent skill to have. Most people assume that because I was an actress, I'm great at public speaking, but I'm not. Being given lines to memorize and act out as someone else — that I can do. I find that easy. But public speaking is a whole other matter. By the way, on a side note, doesn't it piss you off when people miss-speak and say "nother", like *public speaking is a whole nother matter*? Sorry, had to get that out.

Getting up and creating a cohesive speech with a solid introduction, body, and conclusion while staying on topic is hard. Most people don't listen to what they're saying when they talk and when you add nerves into that bundle, people fall apart. Also, most people don't know what to do with themselves when they stand up to talk so that doesn't help.

47

I used to dance when I was younger. I did ballet, tap and jazz. Recitals where we danced on stage as a group were easy — no nerves. It didn't matter that the auditorium was packed, it didn't really bother me. But when I was older (like eleven), I started baton twirling and would go to competitions. With those, we would be solo, competing in front of entire gymnasiums of onlookers and a panel of judges. *That* was nerve-wracking. Sweaty palms and weak knees are not the best equation for a solid performance, especially when you are expected to toss up a metal baton (very slippery with sweaty hands) and do spins, cartwheels or walkovers before catching it again. So those were a challenge.

I am a relatively new member of Toastmasters. Toastmasters is a club that provides a supportive environment in which to practice public speaking skills. They have a program that you can work through at your own pace (ten speeches with various required elements to become a Distinguished Toastmaster (DTM). Then, there are leadership programs you can pursue). The clubs also have Table Topics at every meeting. Table Topics are given out randomly to members and they have one to two minutes to answer them. The goal is to develop the skill of on-the-spot public speaking and increase confidence…which is the ultimate goal.

Public speaking skills are not debatable. You either have them or you don't. It's not something you can really fake. As scary as public speaking is…I really like that about it. Think about it, public speaking is hard but it's also something that you can learn. Yes, it's true that some people are born with the gift of gab. In the NIM competition, Thor Schrock had it and it gave him a distinct advantage over some of the other contestants because no matter what, no matter whether he knew what he was talking about or not, he could talk for hours and sound like an expert. The bullshit gift. I have it with small crowds, I have it with writing, but I don't have it public speaking…yet. I'm working on it.

So here are some public speaking tips I've learned from both Toastmasters and acting:

» **Talk about what you know**. Try to use personal stories or subjects you know well to get your point across. You're more at ease when you're comfortable with the subject.

» Try to **look at each and every audience member when you're talking** to them. This will make them feel like you're talking specifically to them and they'll care more about what you have to say.

» I know this might sound contradictory to the previous tip, but **concentrate on your message... not the audience**. Try to forget they're there.

» **Never apologize!** If you forget something, don't say "I'm sorry," or "Oops, I screwed up." Just move forward. Most times the audience won't even notice your error... they don't know what you're planning to say. But even if it's something that they would notice, don't slap them in the face further with it by apologizing. If you start off by saying something like "I'm sorry, I suck at public speaking, bear with me...," then your audience will already be thinking you're not very good because that's what you told them to think.

» Have someone **count your fillers** (i.e. words like "um," "ah," "like," "you know," "so"). You sound way more professional without filler words. Just take pauses if you're thinking about what comes next.

» **Videotape your practice sessions or performances**, standing up, so you can see your body movements. Most people do things like rock from side to side, shift constantly, put their hands behind their backs, etc. Find your clutches and work on them.

» When you know your clutches, **ask a friend** to point them out. It will help you pay attention.

» Above all else... try to **RELAX**. Know that your audience wants you to succeed. Nobody is hoping you fall flat on your face.

» **Practice!** It's hard to practice public speaking, and I know this might sound incredibly stupid, but you can always do something like flip through the dictionary or a book, find a word or phrase, and ask yourself a question. Then formulate an answer, stand up and give it. This works better with two or more people, but you can do it alone. It helps with structure and confidence.

When I was dancing, we'd videotape both practice sessions and performances. Sometimes we think we're doing something and we're not. For example, with dancing, it's so important to point your toes during kicks or cartwheels. I always thought I was doing that, and whenever somebody would yell "Jaime, point your toes!", I would think "I am — shut up." But then I would see the video and I couldn't deny it.

As soon as I'd heard we would be public speaking, the first cohesive thought that entered my brain was "Why have I not been attending my Toastmasters meetings?" Because really, that's what this challenge was — a Table Topics question. *Tell me why so-and-so should be the Next Internet Millionaire.* Bam — intro, body, conclusion — done.

Easy, peasy, right? Yeah right.

I was paired up with Jason Marshall. Since we didn't really know each other yet, I was not confident in speaking easily in front of these people. Plus, this challenge mattered. Whoever won wasn't going home.

50

We had about five minutes in total to get info from each other. Then we were called up one by one to present.

I thought I had what I was going to say down pat. But it sort of got jumbled up when I actually stood up to say it. In fact, I Homer Simpson-ed it. As fans of the show will remember, there were two Jasons in this competition. I kept telling myself "do not say Jason Henderson, do not say Jason Henderson." And what do I say when I get up there… well, if you guessed that I said "Jason Henderson" at the end of my speech, you would be dead on. Doh!

Other than that, I thought I did a decent job. Both Thor and Jason Marshall stood out as strong public speakers to me — and Jason Marshall won the Hacker Safe Immunity for the day. Oh well — at least he was talking about me.

I want to share my favourite song about public speaking that I feel totally captures the feeling. It's "Lose Yourself" by Eminem. The whole song's great, but I'm only going to share the first bit:

Look, if you had one shot or one opportunity

To seize everything you ever wanted in one moment

Would you capture it or just let it slip?

Verse 1

His palms are sweaty, knees weak, arms are heavy

There is vomit on his sweater already

Moms forgettin' he's nervous

But on the surface he looks calm and ready

To drops bombs, but he keeps on forgetting

What he wrote down, the whole crowd goes so loud

He opens his mouth but the words won't come out

51

He's choking, how? Everybody's jokin' now

The clock's run out, time's up, over BLOW!

Snap back to reality, oh there goes gravity…

Pretty good, huh?

After the public speaking, lunch was served while the crew tore down the set and built up the next one (the Classroom). Our waiting/working area set was a nice couch with blankets, a massage chair (very nice — and absolutely necessary), games (Chess, Rubik's Cube, Sudoku), a table and chairs… it was very nice and comfy.

We were all so full from breakfast that no one really wanted to eat the lunch. Kaitlyn came up to us and pleaded that we go get something because the food had been donated and it would look really bad if we didn't eat anything. So we went up and took a bit to be polite. I didn't eat anything, maybe just a piece of fruit. I realized later that I should have loaded up regardless of how hungry I was. In fact, that sort of became my motto as the competition went on. Eat when you can, because you never know when and what you'll eat next.

I'm sure we did more interviews/confessionals. I felt badly for the crew. They were trying hard to get us to give dirt on the other contestants. I don't know what the others said and did in their confessionals… but I don't think I gave them much. I know now, after watching the show, that some contestants felt quite comfortable dishing.

After lunch we were ushered into the Classroom to hear Mark Joyner speak.

Mark Joyner is widely recognized as one of the early pioneers of e-commerce. The guy basically invented eBooks. He is a number 1 best-selling author of over a dozen books that have been translated in many languages. And he's a Cold War veteran of military intelligence and a former U.S. Army Officer (he even had Top Secret SCI clearance, the highest clearance level in the US) for many years. That means the guy probably knows, in addition to all the web marketing stuff, who killed Kennedy. But seriously, Mark's a good guy… and he looks like The Rock (not Alcatraz, the actor/wrestler).

Mark talked to us about Simple.ology. Simple.ology is the simple science of getting what you want. In my opinion, Simple.ology is a really great online time management tool. It will get you wherever you want to go faster and with the least possible effort.

Simple.ology helps you plan clearly and simply how to bridge the gap between your dreams and reality.

How?

Well, there are five laws of Simple.ology.

The first law of Simple.ology is the law of straight lines. The shortest path between where you are and where you want to go in life is a straight line. The problem is that most of us don't follow that line. We're all over the place. What Mark is talking about is common sense, really. We, as people, actually know this…we just don't follow it most of the time.

> *"Insanity: doing the same thing over and over again and expecting different results."*
>
> ~Albert Einstein

The second law of Simple.ology is the law of clear vision. To hit a target/goal, you have to see it clearly.

Imagine being blindfolded and trying to play darts. How many times do you think you'd even hit the board?

Again, this is common sense stuff, that's why I'm sure Mark called his product Simple.ology — hey, it's *simple*. But just because it's simple, doesn't mean we actually do it.

"I wanna be super-rich" isn't a clear target. Exactly how much money do you want to have and when? "I want to be happy." Okay great — what makes you happy? What defines your happiness? What marks this success?

A stronger/clearer target might be… "I want to open my own retail clothing store and have profited seventy-five thousand dollars by the end of the second year." Now you have a clear target and you can start working backwards on the exact steps that will help you achieve that goal.

The third law of Simple.ology is the law of focused energy. In order to hit a target, you must focus sufficient energy on it until you hit it.

That's huge because often we focus on the wrong things.

This is like what I mentioned earlier about Homer Simpson and saying Jason Henderson's name in the Hacker Safe Immunity Challenge instead of Jason Marshall's. I had been focusing on "don't say Jason Henderson, don't say Jason Henderson." Hello? What did I say? Jason Henderson, because that's what I had been focusing on.

You can also focus on distractions that pull you away from your goal. "I'm really craving chocolate." "I just want to watch this show, " or "I should get on Facebook."

I am the best procrastinator in the world. Anything and everything can pull me away from my goal so this Simple.ology law is one I really have to work on in order to achieve success.

The fourth law of Simple.ology is the law of focused attention. In order to accomplish something, you have to focus sufficient attention on it until you've done it.

54

Many times people fail simply because they don't focus enough attention to their goals. It might be that they give up too soon — that happens a lot. If you've planned out your steps properly, you should clearly see bit by bit what you need to do. That, alone, should keep your energy focused.

The fifth law of Simple.ology is the inescapability of Action/Reaction.

You can never escape action and reaction. Even if you don't know it, you are always acting. And acting causes a reaction. If you're deciding what to do, you're acting — your action is "deciding". If you're procrastinating — that's your action.

Time passes by quickly and it's your biggest commodity. You can't get it back. If you are watching TV instead of working towards your goal — that time is gone. That action of procrastination has now caused the reaction of time passed with you no closer to that goal. If you are also munching away at popcorn while you are procrastinating with a movie, now you have added the reaction of feeling sick and sluggish to your waste of time.

Whatever you do means something.

Those are the laws of Simple.ology and I think they make a lot of sense.

I mean, basically, to succeed you have to think differently than everybody else because, think about it, most people fail.

By using Simple.ology software, you can fill in your goals and dreams. The software helps you list step by step how you'll accomplish these goals. It's basically about picturing the end result and working backwards, carefully, so you don't miss a step. By doing this, by making sure you capture every little step, **you will accomplish your goals — and faster**. Because you're not wasting time.

55

We also learned that every day you should do your Daily Target Praxis, for which you use the Simple.ology software. To do this:

» Go to a quiet location;

» Get rid of distractions (email, IM, phone);

» Make sure you're not surrounded by clutter;

» Clear your mind of everything except your major targets;

» Brain dump useless items (by writing down — the brain can only remember so much information, so if you get the useless stuff (phone calls, errands, etc.) out, you'll be able to focus more);

» Next, you'll do a daily exercise (example: writing down your "time leeches", things you do that suck away your time);

» Next, you'll do your power praxis of the day (like removing the leeches);

» Then you'll review your major targets (short-term, medium-term and long-term). You'll see yourself hitting them. Imagine how you'll feel when you accomplish them. And realize that accomplishing these goals will bring you closer to your ultimate dreams.

Exercises like the Daily Target Praxis help to keep you on track.

Simple.ology is free — you should check it out at www.simple-ology.com. You can buy up on the product… but, like I said, the basics are free and they can really help you out.

Time management and trying to follow a straight line is huge. HUGE.

There have been so many things I've wanted in my life that I haven't accomplished because I didn't plan properly. Because I didn't plan, I missed steps. After hearing Mark speak, I wanted to

56

slap myself. God — if I had followed the Simple.ology philosophy, who knows where I'd be right now?

You can be sure I wouldn't be working in a job I hate. You can be sure I would have found a way to do whatever I wanted.

When I put together the musical audition for NIM, or my short film Anonymous, I followed steps. I knew what I wanted as the end result and I walked backwards slowly and looked at everything. And, guess what? I did it.

I WALKED BACKWARDS THROUGH THE PROJECTS IN ADVANCE AND SUCCEEDED IN DOING WHAT I WANTED TO DO.

Hmmmmm......

Now I can think of a number of times that I didn't plan properly... and **it can be about anything in life**, not just business.

What proper planning could work for:

» Wanting to lose weight

» Getting in shape

» Buying a house

» Saving up for a Cooper Mini (hey — it's my favourite car!)

» Cleaning up your room

» Becoming a better public speaker

» Writing a novel

» Learning French

» Becoming the richest person in the world

Are you getting the picture? I know I'm starting to sound like a sales letter here, but I'm just getting excited. And, having just finished off a bucket of gummy worms, I'm probably more than a bit sugar-rushed. (I'll talk about health later, but, since I haven't yet, you can't get down on my sugar habit.)

Okay, back to the Classroom...

After Mark finished talking we got a short break, which we all seriously needed. I think the producers forgot the simple equation of: extreme heat + extra H20 + 2 hour time period = SERIOUS NEED TO PEE.

With all the stage lights for the cameras, it was so, so hot in the Classroom. It was putting some people to sleep (against their will, of course). I am really pretty good with heat. I love it. I always tell people that I'm solar-powered (I *need* the sun). And I'm usually cold in a room when others are hot. So, let me tell you, this room was hot. If I'm hot in a room, I always feel sorry for the other people. And I was hot. I felt like I was going to spontaneously combust. Seriously. It was beyond sweating hot. It was explode hot. I don't know how these gurus did it in suits.

So, since this wasn't the Judgement Room, the contestants had been given glasses of water. Well, for me it became a challenge to see how long I could last without drinking the water during these classroom sessions. I'd wait to see how long I could remain parched, and when I was almost dying, I'd take a sip. Because, you couldn't just put up your hand and say "Hey, I'm about to explode." You had to wait until they called a bathroom break. And we never knew when that was going to happen.

They also, I should mention, only had one Men's and one Women's bathroom in the COMMplex. Every time they called a bathroom break, all twelve contestants would run for the bathroom, but with six and six of the genders (plus crew), it could take quite a while. That was one benefit of the later days of competition — less people, less wait time. Yes, I know, I'm a girl who really focuses on the important stuff.

After the pee break, we were back in the Classroom. This time we were being given our Execution Challenge of the day. The winning team would be immune, the losing team would have to go to the Judgement Room where two of its team members would be eliminated. Two!

Teams were picked. Jason Marshall was one team captain. He selected Debbie to be the other. They picked teams alternating genders. I was not the first to be picked — can't say that didn't hurt my feelings (but I'm always insulted when people don't think I'm a first-round pick — probably everyone is. Aren't you?). Anyway, I ended up on Jason's team and we picked K.I.S.S. (**K**eep **I**t **S**imple **S**tupid) as our team name. The other team picked Bullseye.

KISS players: Jason Marshall, Alisande Chan, Steve Schuitt, Laura Martin, Jason Henderson and me.

Bullseye players (the remainder of the contestants — okay, I'll spell them out): Debbie Ducic, Charles Trippy, Carly Taylor, Christine Schaap, Thor Schrock and Nico Pasani.

Our challenge was to create a new landing page (squeeze page) for Simple.ology. A landing page, for those of you who don't know, is a page where you get your customers to commit to your product. With Simple.ology, it's free to join, but still, to get people to join is not always easy. People don't like to put their information down in your system. They don't want to be hit constantly with spam emails. They don't want their information sold to lists. They don't know whether or not they even *want* your product. What will it do for them? What is the benefit to them to give you their information down?

We needed to create a fifteen minute presentation, utilizing all of our team members, describing our new page.

And we had two and a half hours to put the whole thing together.

59

We were sequestered to our work areas. There was a lot to think about. First, we had to pick our target market. We had to look at what they were doing now and do something different, because, obviously, if they want something new, what they have isn't giving them the desired results. We then needed to design a new page. That new page needed new, grabbing copy. Then we needed to plan out our presentation and rehearse it.

Our team split into departments. Alisande and I worked on the new copy and headline. Copywriting is essential, and luckily we both had a knack for it, but we both have different writing styles so it was interesting to work together.

Luckily I have had the opportunity to do InSights Discovery. A couple of years ago, my section at the government did this one-day course. It was an amazing eye-opener in my life and helped me tremendously in working with other people.

Before you go to the course, they email you a test of twenty-five questions. Based on your answers to those questions (and the questions themselves might vary based on your answers to the previous questions, I don't know), but based on your answers, they put together an extensive personality profile for you based on a four-color system: Red, Yellow, Blue and Green.

And, boy, are they accurate. About ten of us took the course that day, and every single one of us was shocked with how much our booklets described our personalities. We even read each other's booklets after the course to make sure that it wasn't one of those horoscope-type things where they're so general that any of them could work on anybody. No way. These were accurate and detailed.

The twenty page booklets list:

>> Your personal style

>> How you interact with others

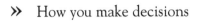

» How you make decisions

» Your key strengths and weaknesses

» How you are a value to a team

» How effective you are at communicating

» Your possible blind spots

» How to communicate with your opposite type

» Suggestions for development

» Your ideal environment

» How to manage and motivate you

» Your management style

As you can see, it's pretty intensive. And oh so right!

This type of testing is solidly based on the pioneering personality profiling work of Dr. Carl Jung.

The tests find out which color personality you are. We are all a mixture of the four different colors and everybody's mix is different. That's why everybody's booklet is totally them, it's not just a *red* book, a *yellow* book — you get the point.

If **red** is your strongest color:

» You may be seen as assertive and forthright

» You are action-oriented and always in motion

» You are strong-willed, reality-oriented and focused on the achievement of results and objectives

» You will approach others in a direct, authoritative manner, radiating a desire to control and conclude

» You may become aggressive and overbearing

61

» You may be viewed as impatient and controlling

» You may sometimes appear dismissive of others and more concerned with the task than the people

» You respond well to immediate challenges

» You have great certainty that the task can be achieved

» You inject energy and a sense of urgency into the group

If **yellow** is your strongest color:

» You tend to be seen as outgoing, radiant and friendly

» You are usually positive and concerned with establishing good human relations

» You enjoy the company of others and believe that life should be fun

» You approach others in a persuasive, democratic manner, radiating a desire to enjoy and discover

» Under pressure, you may become excitable and frantic

» Your heightened desire for inclusion may cause you to become indiscreet and act in a way that is inappropriate for the situation

» You may struggle with self-organisation and miss deadlines

» You provide humour and lighten up the proceedings

» You show excitement for new ideas and take others with you

» You believe that anything is possible

If **blue** is your strongest color:

» You will tend to be seen as self-contained

» You will have a desire to know and understand the world around you

» You like to think before you act and maintain a detached, objective standpoint

» You value independence and intellect

» Your need for clarity and precision means you tend to prefer written communication to the spoken word, radiating a desire to analyse and understand

» You may become over-concerned with the detail and too immersed in the process

» Others may view you as aloof or even cold

» You question ideas and ensure thorough research takes place

» You ensure that tasks are reviewed and that lessons are learned for next time

» You ensure details are not overlooked

If **green** is your strongest color:

» You tend to be seen as concerned about values and depth in relationships

» You want others to be able to rely on you

» You will defend what you value with a quiet determination and persistence

» You prefer democratic relations that recognise the individual and are personal in style, radiating a desire to appreciate and support

» You may become defiant and stubborn, even obstructive

63

» Others may see you as someone who is too willing to appease and who wishes to maintain harmony at any cost

» Others may believe you lack the ability to make a clear decision

» You listen to everyone's contribution

» You see both sides in times of conflict and attempt to retain synergy

» You can be a good sounding board for individuals

» You consider the impact on others when decisions are being made

The levels of each of your colors describe exactly who you are. The order of my colors is red, yellow, blue and green (that is why I chose to list them that way).

Learning who you are and what other personalities are like is so valuable to life and success.

LIFE LESSON 3: Learn who you are and how to work with other personalities.

I worked with this one woman in the government and we did not get along at all. She was strong-minded but never spoke up in meetings. She knew things, but it would take her forever to analyze the situation. She needed to be clear before she spoke. And speaking wore her out. She was also very detailed and process-oriented. She was very different from me — I didn't get her and she didn't get me. Through taking the course, I believe we learned quite a bit about the other person so that, although we never liked each other, we learned to work together. Which is really what it's all about.

Okay — back to the competition…

In the end, our presentation won over that of Bullseye and we didn't have to go into the Judgement Room, thank God.

Our team was starving. Supper had been served while we were working, as a tactic to see if we'd be distracted. Well we hadn't been, but that meant we were now in serious need of food.

While the other team was being judged, we snacked on veggies and tried to stay awake. It was getting pretty late and we'd had an early start.

When the Bullseye team emerged, it was an ugly sight. They had been mentally beaten up, every single one of them. I don't know what went on in that room, but they were a solemn crowd. Even Charles, who'd said he'd really just come to the competition as a joke, was sobered up. Carly and Debbie had been put in The Sandbox (they could now only watch and not participate).

It was finally time to go back to the hotel. There were no individual suites anymore. Laura, Carly and I were sharing. It was after midnight — there would be no partying for me. To bed.

{ ARMAND MORIN }

DAY 2 AND

D ay two of the competition began with the Hacker Safe Immunity Challenge. Today's guest judge for the challenge was Joshua Sloan from 1 and 1 (1and1.com). 1 and 1 is considered the world's number one web hosting company. And Joshua seems like a very genuine man. He puts in that extra effort to make sure you're getting what you need from 1 and 1.

Today we're focusing on their blog department: 1and1 Blog!

A blog is a website where entries are written in chronological order and commonly displayed in reverse chronological order. "Blog" can also be used as a verb, meaning to maintain or add content to a blog.

Blogs provide commentary or news on a particular subject such as food, politics, or local news; some function as more personal online diaries. A typical blog combines text, images, and links to other blogs, web pages, and other media related to its topic. The ability for readers to leave comments in an interactive format is an important part of many blogs. Most blogs are primarily textual, although some focus on art (artlog), photographs (photoblog), sketchblog, videos (vlog), music (MP3 blog), audio (podcasting) or sexual topics (Adult blog), and are part of a wider network of social media.

67

In May 2007, blog search engine Technorati was tracking more than 71 million blogs.

~**Wikipedia** (*a free online encyclopedia*)

1 and 1 Blog is a personal publishing medium that is included free with all shared hosting packages. It's really quick — it can be installed in two minutes and with no programming skills (although from my limited experience, if you have some, you're better off).

A great feature of 1 and 1 Blog is that there are a number of customizable templates to choose from so you can make your blog your own. And they have free 24/7 support which is always cool.

The challenge was to create a blog using 1 and 1 Blog and populate it with content. We had to remove some of the basic templating and make it a bit more our own and we had to write over two hundred and fifty words. We had one hour.

Oh — and now for the real challenge… a random topic was chosen from each contestant's bio and put in a hat. We had to draw from the hat to know what our blog was going to be about!

Laura and Christine got lucky and picked their own topics.

I picked Computer Repair (Thor's)!

What the hell do I know about computer repair? Nothing, that's what. That's why I'm ready to throw my computer in the garbage whenever the simplest thing is wrong with it. I just don't know and don't have the patience. So this was a horrible topic for me.

And that hour of work time we were being given INCLUDED our research time. Nice.

Using the 1 and 1 Blog templates was relatively easy. Given more time and research on what makes a good blog (since I never go to any, I really had no clue), I could have created a master-piece. But I did what I had time to do.

Next was researching computer repair. Oh my god — I just glazed over. The subject is just so boring for me (sorry Thor and any other tech person reading this). And if I'm going to write about something, it has to interest me. Otherwise it's like writing a report for school — strained.

I had an idea about how to twist the subject into something more my style. I decided to write my blog in kind of a chick-lit way (very Sex and the City). I started it off (and I'm going to put my whole first post down here — don't worry it's not that long, and then I'll talk about writing) …

Computer Repair —
My computer dumped me… HELP!

Are computers male? This is my question.

I thought I had the perfect relationship with my laptop. I kept it streak free and dust free. I carried it around like it was a pair of Manolo Blaniks. I even bought it a gorgeous leather carry bag — in navy blue, of course.

Let me give you some background… my laptop and I started our relationship two years ago. I was thrilled. Like every woman, I have a list of what I am looking for in a companion and my laptop was perfection.

We were going strong… he treated me like a queen. He did everything I asked without talking back. I fell in love.

All of my past computers were junky, they were the bad boys, but not this one.

Then, out of the blue, wham! He shut me out. What did I do? I racked my brain, I couldn't think of anything. I tried restarting to reboot the hard drive. You know, sometimes a laptop really just needs to be turned on. But that didn't work. The screen was gone. Our relationship was over without warning.

So what did I do??

Like every girl... I fought. There was no way I was going to let him walk out of my life. Plus... he had my stuff.

All of my files, my photos, my videos. He stole them and wasn't giving them back.

It was then I decided to seek out help. The computer repair shop, a.k.a. my relationship counsellor, said I should bring him in. I booked an appointment.

My paunchy-looking counsellor with large glasses came out and gave me the diagnosis — my hard drive, corrupted. I was shattered. Again I asked "what did I do?"

Apparently I did nothing. Hard drives can just die.

I started to cry... can I ever get my stuff back?? What about my photos from Mexico??

You backed up your files, right, he asked? What? No... nobody told me! Oops.

I ended up writing two posts. The second was titled: A New Independent Woman — Hear Me Roar. There I talk about getting on with my life and what I learned about hard drives and what I can do (if anything) to prevent problems in the future.

Writing is easy. There, I said it. But guess what? Writing is also very hard.

Does that make any sense?

If you're confused, that's okay. I think most writers are.

There are always fundamentals that are important when you write:

» Spelling (although misspelling words can be cool — search engines don't pick them up, so they not only make you look stupid, they hurt your business)

» Grammar (make sure you have your "your" and "you're" down, amongst other common grammatical errors)

» Be clear

» Be concise

» Use short words, short sentences and short paragraphs

» Unless you're writing policy documents, write in a conversational tone (it's easier to read and understand)

Some people like to really plan out what they're going to write. I've tried it both ways.

When I wrote my first screenplay, I wrote all my points down on cue cards and wrote from those, tossing each one away as I finished that point.

For my second screenplay, I took each of my four main characters and wrote out pages and pages of their back-stories. Where were they born? Where did they go to school? How were they as children? Were they popular? Were they fussy? I wrote down every little detail about them and their families so that I had constructed solid people. I knew them inside and out so that when it became time to write the story, I just saw it unfold before my eyes… I didn't need to write cue card notes.

Next I tried the "hey — I have no idea what direction I'm going with this" approach. Funnily enough, I think this one actually works best for me; the non-focused approach. I know where I

71

ultimately want my characters to end up, but I have absolutely no way of knowing how they're going to get there... and that's okay, because it just unfolds. The characters take charge.

I write as if I'm watching a movie. For me, the most difficult part about writing is picking a character's name. Once I have his or her name — I know them. I have no idea if that makes any sense, but that's what I do.

I actually have a list of names — I suppose it would have been easier to just buy a book of names, but I actually thought for about two weeks of every name I could think of and made an Excel spreadsheet. I scour that sheet and make a narrowed down list and finally choose. It's a process that can take hours, but then I write the entire script in two weeks — very strange.

I lose myself in my writing whether I'm writing for a blog, like in the challenge, or writing scripts. I find myself immersed in the story. I actually forget what I've written once it's on paper (in the computer). It's seriously weird, I know. But I do. Often, I'll go back and look at things a few weeks later, read them and think "Wow, this is really good — did I write this?".

Earlier this year, I was involved in a twenty-four hour playwriting contest. The players were given four specific elements that had to appear in the play (to try and prevent people using pre-written scripts). I wrote a thirty-three-page play that I was really happy with.

About a month later, I was at my friend's house and picked up a play sitting on the coffee table. I started reading it. "Hey — I'm liking this... wait a minute... hey, wait a minute. I WROTE THIS." Yeah, I might be crazy. I don't know. That's okay; everybody who is interesting is at least a bit crazy, right? Or maybe that's just something my mother told me so I wouldn't feel bad about myself.

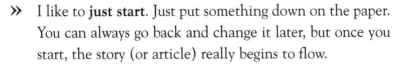

» I like to **just start**. Just put something down on the paper. You can always go back and change it later, but once you start, the story (or article) really begins to flow.

» **Focus/concentrate**. If you're someone who needs distractions, that's fine, just make sure they're in the background. Go to Starbucks. Play some music. I like to write in silence. I don't know why, but distractions pull me out of the story. Your ideal writing environment might be completely different. The important thing is to recognize what you need, then go for it and start writing.

» **Motivate yourself by setting guidelines**. "I'm going to write a paragraph." "I'm going to write for a half an hour." I guarantee you that most times you'll go way over. When I was finishing my first novel in New York, each day I made myself agree to write five pages before leaving my friend's apartment and heading out on the town. This was my holiday in New York and I stayed in and wrote, you guessed it, way more than five pages each day because I got so involved.

» **Try new things**. I always write about different things. My characters are different ages, different sexes. I like changing things up. It broadens your knowledge too.

» **Be open to edits**. The worst thing a writer can do is be too protective of their work. Of course we are all proud of what we write — it's a huge accomplishment. But you have to be humble and realize that you are writing to please other people, not yourself. Everybody's going to have an opinion — once I realized that, my life became a whole lot easier. That's not to say you should let people push you around. But you should be open to hearing

DAY 2 AND ARMAND MORIN

suggestions and then really think about them. And, if you can, try to get an editor that you really trust. That way, when they make suggestions, you know they're valid.

» This one is cheesy, I know… but **have fun.**

Actually getting your work published is very difficult, but if you want to write, WRITE. So many people talk about writing but never do it. And you know what? You never know what will happen. I have so many unpublished manuscripts, and then I entered an audition for a reality show. Now I'm being published and it will open the door to future publishing deals (pretty please).

As for the challenge, my writing got the most laughs (and that's why I wrote it), but I didn't win the challenge, Charles Trippy did. He linked a video up to his and did a good job.

Joel came up to me afterwards and told me I did a great job. He said that I was so close… and that I surprised him. I guess that was a good thing — score one for me.

Armand Morin was our afternoon Classroom guru. He is one of the most well known Internet marketers in the world today. Seriously, he knows his stuff. His personal online businesses have produced over twenty-five million dollars in online revenue. I'm just going to repeat that… **$25,000,000.00.** Cool or cool?

Armand teaches Internet business building principles and strategies that work, without fail, for every single business who has implemented them (so it sounds like people should hear him speak). And, not surprisingly, he appears at live business trainings and seminars all over the world.

On this afternoon, Armand spoke to us mostly about branding. He teaches that you want/need to develop a brand for your company. AND THAT BRAND SHOULD NOT BE YOU. This is because associating your name with your company means that it is very hard to distance yourself from it. For example, what if I created this great online video company where people could upload their videos for everybody to watch and comment on… and I called it Jaime Luchuck Videos? I don't think it's as appetizing to a company like Google, for instance, or You Tube because the purchaser will have greater difficulty promoting that company with an actual other person's name on it. The name "You Tube," on the other hand, isn't identifiable with any one person. You get the picture?

Picking a name for your company is very difficult. The name should be obvious. What Armand did is decide on a branding of "generator". So, every product he creates has "generator" in it. He has "Software Generator", "eBook Generator", "Sales Letter Generator"… you follow?

You want to keep your name short. Basically a key word and an adjective or action. Or a phrase that describes your company (but only two to three words). You should also avoid numbers or dashes. As well as strange names that are misspelled, like my dad's company that I mentioned earlier, Cre84u. If your customers can't spell your business name (even though it's really clever), they aren't finding you (sorry dad).

And never use negative words in your brand.

You should also try to create a name using words that create a visual. After all, you are going to have to have a logo.

If you're having problems deciding… or you just want to see what's successful in your market, CHECK OUT YOUR COMPETITION.

LIFE LESSON 4: You should always know exactly what your competition is doing… and do it better.

Obviously, it's really hard to compete with a super-famous brand name, but try to offer your customers a different experience. Think of something they (your competition) are not giving your customers — and give it to them. I'll get into this more with another guru, but basically, use your competitors' business models to give you ideas. Are the successful people using certain colors? Are their website layouts similar?

Once you have your brand… stay consistent. Keep the style of your website, sales letter, and auto-responders consistent. If you have a storefront shop, keep your window design, your bags, and your newspaper or magazine advertisements consistent.

Did you know… women judge a website in less than five seconds (hey — I know, we're judgemental); with men, it's ten seconds. That's why branding is so important. In five seconds, you see the look and feel and logo. And name recognition brings comfort (go consistency).

So, even though I know you know this, I'm going to say it anyway… FIRST IMPRESSIONS ARE CRUCIAL.

Again, this stuff makes sense. It's not hard. And that's what I like about the concepts.

Lesson done… it was time for our Execution Challenge.

Tonight's challenge was to create a new logo (branding) for *The Next Internet Millionaire*. This logo would appear on a t-shirt, promoting the show.

Since the teams were now off balance, Bullseye was allowed to select one of our members. They picked Jason Marshall to come over to their team, hoping to hurt us by stealing our "leader".

We were asked to select a team captain. Every single member of my team said "Jaime" at the same time. I guess that meant it would be me. Don't get me wrong, I like leading (okay, I love being in charge), but if your team loses, the leader would be a strong target to go. Just look at Day One's elimination.

But, I'm a graphics girl. I was confident with the challenge. I've created company logos before. But there was an unpleasant surprise… we had to create these logos using kindergarten supplies. We had Bristol board, paint, markers, fabric, stained glass. No pencils or pens.

AND NO ONE ON OUR TEAM WAS ARTISTIC.

This was not good. Photoshop I love. Photoshop I can use. Photoshop I know like the back of my hand. But, put a marker in my hand and I can barely draw a stick-figure, let alone a professional looking logo for Joel Comm's reality show.

But first things first, we had to brainstorm ideas. Brainstorming is great. When I brainstorm, I find it easiest to talk about key words as a group, then go off individually and sketch out some ideas. This means that everybody on the team can participate and it won't be a team led by the bossiest people.

That's the worst, when you have people on a team who are so sure that their ideas are the best that they won't/don't listen to anybody else's. Then you have the quiet shy people, who aren't really confident with their ideas, and they get lost, pushed around by the loud-mouths.

So that's what we did for the first part. Alisande, Laura, Steve and I were busy sketching. I came up with some ideas that I really liked. They were simple and straightforward.

Then I had us pitch the ideas. One of our team members was quite forceful (pushy) with ideas and felt like theirs was the only option. I didn't particularly agree, but decided to have a democratic team. We voted and the team picked that design. So, at least we had a design. In these kind of competition settings, there isn't much time, so when you have an idea, you get to work.

Leading teams is a tricky thing.

There are two styles of leadership:

» Authoritarian

- The leader makes all the decisions
- The team is task-oriented
- The team is governed by policy and structure
- The leader is considered the expert

» Facilitative

- The leader works for a consensus from team members
- The leader uses intrinsic motivation (praise, etc.)
- The leader encourages the empowerment of team members to solve problems and make decisions

If, as a team leader, you are trying to encourage participation from your team members, you should ask them questions. Open-ended questions are the best for getting people to join in and share their ideas.

Be careful of the body language you, as a team leader, are using. Crossing your arms and not smiling does not encourage facilitation.

Remember, a team is smarter than any one person. But you have to set up an environment that encourages all team members to express their thoughts and ideas. You want buy-in from all your members or you won't have a strong team.

There are four types of team members.

The **Mummy** will not participate freely in group discussions. Likely introverted or unconfident, they will shy away from putting their ideas on the table and often get bullied into stronger members' positions.

The **Windbag** is likely the first person to speak on any issue. They tend to comment too frequently and often dominate the discussions.

The **Rambler** will often get side-tracked. They might start talking about something completely different from the task or joke around. Often, they will also use low-probability or far-fetched examples to make a point.

The **Homesteader** is a person who takes an initial position and is highly reluctant to budge or consider other viable alternatives.

It is my experience that these team-member types cross-over. People can be more than one type.

That said, every category of team member, as well as variations thereof, was represented in our group.

Ultimately, our team lost the challenge. I ended up being satisfied with our design, but Bullseye's looked better. Having art talent on the team was a huge benefit and we just did not have much to show for. If this was a graphic design challenge, you can bet your ass things would have ended up differently.

But it wasn't, so we met the judges in the Judgement Room.

The Judgement Room, as I mentioned earlier, is not the nicest place. It's set up to increase the dramatic effect for viewers. Five of us went in and we knew that only three were coming out. Luckily, the Hacker Safe Immunity winner was not on our team that day.

A good businessperson can choose who he wants to work with, who he doesn't, and know why. This must be Joel's theory behind the step of asking the contestants who they think should be eliminated from the team.

It's a good theory — people should be able to make decisions and speak their mind. However, it's not a fun thing to do... and it's not like we'll never see each other again. You might pick someone to go home, tell everyone why, and then they might stay... how's that for making friends?

As the team leader, I had to choose first. Joel had complimented me on my leadership style and had also pointed out that he saw my sketches and had liked them. I didn't think I was going.

But I felt uncomfortable picking my team-mates, even though I was fully aware of the two people I thought should go based on the performances. Unfortunately, and I still can't figure out why, I didn't pick the two people I thought should go.

My first pick to go... was myself.

LIFE LESSON 5: Never pick yourself to take the fall.

I now know a better way to have handled that situation would have been to pick the other two, but we're trained in society that the captain goes down with the ship. Well, don't do it Captain — get on that lifeboat!

People's real personalities come out in that room. Stress. I heard there were little "I won't vote you off if you don't vote me off" deals going on behind the scenes. I have to admit, I never made any such alliances.

But one of the people on my team voted me as one of the people to leave. Only one person did (other than me, of course). And, after the judges left the room, he leaned over to me and whispered "yeah, that was BS... I didn't know what to tell them so I had to make something up." Yeah, nice. You can imagine how he endeared himself to me. If he honestly believed that I should go, then fine, vote me off. But, come on. If you do something nasty to someone, maybe don't sheepishly apologize for it afterwards. Have some conviction.

Anyway, I didn't go home. Laura and Steve were sent to the Sandbox. I didn't agree with the judges' decision. If I had to pick, I would have replaced one of those two with another team member. How's that for vague? I was safe yet another day… and I was in serious need of sleep.

DAY 3 AND
{ JEFF WALKER }

W hat's the most common-sense activity to do at 9:00 in the morning? Well, if you answered "play poker," I wouldn't have agreed with you. But you would have been right on the money that Wednesday morning.

Now, you should know, right off the bat, that I have no idea how to play poker. You should also know, because I mentioned it earlier, that Alisande had tried to teach a few of us in her hotel room a few nights before. I should have paid closer attention. A lot closer. Little did I know...

My only past experiences with poker have been to play strip poker. I admit that — only because I always dressed up for those occasions by wearing lots of layers. So many that, even though I was a horrible and unlucky player, I was never down to my knickers.

Now, I'm sure you can imagine that I was not thrilled to find out that poker was today's Hacker Safe Immunity Challenge. Alisande is a semi-pro poker player, while I play a mean game of cribbage. Hmmm — I'm sensing a knockout here.

But this is poker and it's all a luck-of-the-cards thing, right?

You've got to know when to hold 'em

Know when to fold 'em

Know when to walk away

And know when to run

83

I listened to "The Gambler" when I was younger. Unfortunately, this morning should have been "A time to run."

We all, except the four Sandbox players who watched from the sidelines, sat down at the professional-looking, green and black poker table. It looked brand new, although I doubt it was. But, somehow, its look of newness reassured me. It seemed less daunting if no sucker had lost his shirt during some random night of debauchery.

The NIM producers had brought in pro dealers and everything. It looked like it was going to be quite a game.

Joel's reasoning for having us play poker was to test our risk analysis skills. In business, you have to be strategic, and by playing this game, apparently he will be able to judge whether or not we possess such skills.

Now, in my opinion, playing a game you know nothing about against others who are quite proficient at it might not be the most strategic move. And, perhaps, it might be a telling sign that you have no risk analysis skills… but I kept those smart-ass comments to myself.

"Roll tape… Action!"

The dealer dealt a hand and explained the rules while we played this round with our cards face-up. And then we were off…

… Now every gambler knows

The secret to survival

Is knowing what to throw away

And knowing what to keep

Cause every hand's a winner

And every hand's a loser…

Well, all I can say to Kenny is that I didn't really get any of those "winner" hands. I lost all my chips before we were even half-way through the game.

You see, I thought, *all-in* (that's where you bet all your chips — yeah, I know, it sounds dumb now) was a good decision. I'm a bit like Marty McFly in *Back To The Future*, I don't like to be called "chicken". Other people had bet "all in", so I thought *Hey, why not?* If I had won, I would have potentially taken the whole game. Perhaps my risk analysis skills could use some help?

I was so, so close. One card away from victory. One card... But close is only good in horseshoes and hand grenades, and I had to leave the table.

The rest of the game, after the crappy players were eliminated, was pretty enjoyable to watch. Tension was a heavyweight in the room — people were sweating... and some were playing to the cameras.

As it turned out, Alisande did not win. I have to admit, I was a little happy about that (sorry Alisande). It was interesting to watch her play, but I usually never vote for the favourite. Plus, she played it a bit too safe for me (listen to me criticize... at least she kept her chips throughout most of the game).

Thor, Jason Marshall, and Nico all knew how to play too, and they played well. Watching how they handled the pressure was really interesting. I guess that's really what Joel was looking to observe. Ultimately, Nico took all the chips and ended the game. He also took the Immunity shirt for the day.

I don't even know what I can say about the poker game that relates to life. The moral in business, I guess, is if you don't know the game, you should learn it before putting your money in. Otherwise, you might as well hand your money over to someone else, and who here likes throwing their money away?

But also, in life, it's good to try new things and not count yourself out from the get-go. That's not always an easy thing to do when you're playing with big-shot players. But sometimes, the best way to get in the pool is to just jump in dry.

Before you say it, I know I just contradicted myself with two cheesy life generalities, but, really, both are true. If you never get in the game, you'll be at your nine-to-five forever. But, on the other hand, if you jump in without doing any research first, you'll go splat and have to crawl back to your boss, on your hands and knees, begging for that crappy job back. Nobody wants to do that.

When I was younger I considered myself a real risk-taker. Before I could even spell, I would write runaway notes to my parents and make plans to leave home (I never got too far — but my parents did get the notes and I did call my grandparents on occasion to make arrangements). In high school, I decided I was bored with my school by the end of Grade 11 and switched for my senior year. That was unheard of. And growing up in a small city (Regina had a population of about 170,000), while everybody talked about "getting out" — I was the first person I knew to actually leave.

Later on, I up and moved to Toronto with no job and nothing in the bank. I worked for Flare magazine for free. I became an actress — my life-long dream.

And then something weird happened… I grew up. Well, I'm not sure you can call it growing up. I think it's more like I grew into my little safe shell of security. It disgusts me to think about it, but it's true.

Now I make excuses for the things I don't do…

I want to move away from Toronto (I have for years), but I haven't. Why? Because I'm set up here. I painted my apartment just the way I like. I have my job (hey — it pays okay). My hairstylist is here and I really like her — she knows my hair. I have some good friends.

What happened to that free spirit? I'm not saying that people should be stupid. Perhaps when I was younger, I was a bit trigger-happy. Maybe moving to a new city with a car full of belongings and zero dollars in the bank is not an ideal situation. But, what I've learned is that, usually, the situation is never ideal. And, if you wait until it is, you'll never go anywhere.

Have you ever thought...

"When I have enough money saved up, then I'll quit my job and do what I want."

"When I lose thirty pounds, then I'll buy those cute jeans and be happy."

"When I'm where I want to be in my career, then I'll take a vacation."

Are you "doing what you want"? "Wearing those cute jeans?" "Vacationing?"

Probably not.

I know someone who is twenty-nine and still lives with her mom and dad. I know someone who is thirty and lives with his mom and dad. 30! Come on. And they are making every safety excuse in the book. Money, company, convenience, time — every excuse they can think of to convince themselves that it's okay. It's not. Take the leap — and get out.

I think you need to weigh every decision in your life. You want to find the balance between being overly carefree and a scared little mouse. New experiences are good (not if you're running away from something though). And getting out of your comfort zone is great!

Back to the Classroom…

Our speaker of the day was Jeff Walker.

For years, Jeff's specialty had been launching new products… and when the fact that he had earned six figures in seven days started to leak out, he became a sought-after "hired gun" for rolling out new promotions. Jeff helps famous and not-so-famous marketers to successfully launch their products, in all kinds of niches.

Here's what I learned about product launches from Jeff:

First of all, you should always check out your competitors. I know I mentioned this before. But this time, make sure you get on their email lists, customer lists… whatever lists they have where they talk about their products. You want to be informed about what they're up to.

By the way, I've been assuming you know this next piece of information, but I'm going to tell you anyway because it deserves repeating:

YOU CAN LAUNCH ANY PRODUCT SUCCESSFULLY.

Jeff has worked with clients in dozens of different niches and, by following his advice, they succeeded with their launches. Some examples of these niche markets are:

» Dating

» Test preparation

» Photoshop tutorials

» Realtors

» Baseball coaches

» Knitting

» Investing

88

» Tax preparation

» Health food

» Business coaching

» Pet care

Basically, your customers need to be affected emotionally or they won't buy from you. There are **twelve mental triggers** you want to hit during a launch.

You see, a product launch is like a novel. You want the tension to build and build until it climaxes. Get your customers interested and keep them interested until the end.

When you are doing a product launch, you are ultimately building a relationship with your potential clients. You're allowing them to get to know you while building their excitement. You might start your launch three or four weeks before your launch day, just to get them drooling.

USE ALL TWELVE MENTAL TRIGGERS IN YOUR LAUNCH.

1 People are more inclined to do something when they see others making that choice. That is called **Social Proof**, and is the first mental trigger. Have you ever noticed how a restaurant will seat customers at the window first? How a night-club will make people stand in line — even though there's room inside the club? How if a celebrity wears an item of clothing, suddenly everybody else is too?

People get worried and scared before making a purchase. If they know that others before them have said "Yes," they'll be more inclined to buy.

89

When I worked at the magazine, we constantly received free items from people who wanted us to feature them (clothing, CD's, books, accessories). Yes, they wanted the advertising. But, mostly, they wanted people to feel that they weren't alone. Flare said it was cool — it must be cool.

How do you get social proof if you can't convince Angelina Jolie to walk around with your product? Well, you need to encourage people to give you testimonials saying that your product is great. That might mean giving some away in exchange for the thumbs-up, or it might mean that you have to offer a bonus in order to get them to spend some time on camera. Get them to talk about how they're going to use your product — what it's going to do for them. Then post those comments on your website so other people can read them.

2 When a limited number of items are available — it's amazing how much quicker people act. That is **Scarcity**. Whether it's that only a certain number will be sold, that the bonuses will go away, or that the first one hundred people get a deal, people will leap at your product to make sure they don't miss out.

And if they do miss out on your deal, as hard as it is, do not bend for them. You might lose out on the sale at that moment… but people talk. And you can be sure, that the next time you advertise, those people AND their friends will make sure they buy when they're given the chance.

I once heard a great story of social proof and scarcity. A speaker said, "Do you want to buy this great red Ferrari for $100,000?. Everybody said "No." "Well," he said, "what if I told you that there were only three of these cars in existence? Would you buy it?" There were some pauses, but eventually people said "No." "Okay. Well, what if I told you that the other two of these cars were owned by Brad Pitt and George Clooney? Would you buy it?" And, guess what? "Yes!" was the answer. Amazing.

3 **Stories** are a great way to sell your product. Tell me about someone who is like me and how your product helped them — and I'll buy. Tell me about someone who is using your product and has the life I want — hey, I'll buy. Maybe I'm a sucker, but stories work.

4 I love Christmas. I love everything about Christmas. But, the most exciting thing about Christmas is the **Anticipation** of Christmas. I love knowing that, come December, I can start playing carols, decorating my house, and shopping. I know that I'll see my family. I have fun wrapping presents in crazy ways so they'll never guess what's inside. (That, by the way, is a family tradition started by my dad. My family is known for one-upping each other in the wrapping department. Christmas morning we might be sent on treasure hunts, be forced to decode a message, or unwrap layer after layer of packing-taped boxes in order to get down to the rock-weighted-down gift.)

In your launch, try to build up anticipation… it's so important.

5 The fifth mental trigger is **Community**. Give people a sense of community, a sense of belonging. Communities influence buying decisions.

6 **Reciprocity** is another trigger. If you give to someone, they'll want to give back to you. Just think about how you feel if someone shows up to your house at Christmas with a gift. How do you feel if you have nothing for them in return?

If you give extras to your customers (and it doesn't have to be products, it could be customer service), you will build loyalty and they will, in turn, want to give back to you.

7 If you are **Consistent**, you will earn the respect of your clients. They might not buy from you the first time, but if you show your potential customers that you are not just in it for the "big sale", that you are consistent in your commitment to quality, they will be more likely to buy.

8 **Controversy** always sells. We've all heard "there is no such thing as bad publicity." It's so true.

9 People want **Proof** that your product is going to do for them what you promise it is. They're not just going to believe you. Why should they?

If you don't have customers already — do a mini-launch to get some success stories.

And proof doesn't have to be about physical products — it could be about you. If you're trying to be a freelance writer (like I was), you're not likely to get a top-notch agent right off the bat. Why would he take you on? You might be good, but you haven't proven you can deliver. Maybe you have one terrific piece, but it might have taken you years to produce it. Agents and editors need to know that you can repeatedly produce quality work. That you're easy to work with. That you, ultimately, get the job done. If you want to get into that business, try sending in letters to the editor. That's being published. That shows that you can write quickly and intellectually.

It shows your shrewdness and wit. By publishing smaller pieces in magazines and papers, you can eventually prove yourself to larger industry people and they won't feel like they're taking a risk.

10 Always give your customers a **Reason Why** they should buy your product. "You want to buy this product *because...*"

11 Create **Interactivity** to generate and boost the excitement. Host an event or get a forum going. People love to participate and that, ultimately, encourages social proof (trigger #1) and community (trigger #5). See how these are starting to feed off each other? Maybe Jeff knows what he's talking about...

12 And, finally, get someone with **Authority** to give your product the thumbs-up. If Oprah says "I recommend Book X. It's amazing," that book immediately shoots up to a best-seller. Need I say more?

But what if you can't get Oprah? Well, try to find somebody in your niche that is considered an expert. Someone that people will recognize. And try to get them to vouch for your product.

When Jeff was done speaking, we were given our Execution Challenge of the day. We were introduced to Wynn Washle, a real estate agent from The Group Inc. in Northern Colorado.

Wynn had been trying to sell a beautiful, unique El Caminito home in Loveland unsuccessfully for a year and a half. Although the home was in a quiet, desired neighbourhood, there had been no bites on the offer.

They had even lowered the price of the house from the $700,000+ range to the $500,000+ range. Nothing.

I almost bought the house right then and there (not that I had the money at the time — but what a steal!). In Toronto, house prices are high. I could barely buy a small bungalow for $500,000 let alone a large three-storey, custom-designed work of art built by an architect.

It was our job to come up with a launch that would sell the home within thirty days.

Again, a subject I know nothing about — real estate. I know you can make a bunch of money off of real estate, but I've never learned how. I rent.

Unfortunately for us, Bullseye had a few members who knew about real estate.

This Execution Challenge was interesting. There were four members of K.I.S.S. (we pulled Jason Marshall back to our team), four members of Bullseye, and the Sandbox team (the four who had been previously banished). If the Sandbox team did not win, they would lose three members. If they won, they would lose two members and the losing team would lose one member. Very interesting from a strategic point of view, and very stressful from the Sandbox team's point of view, I'm sure.

Again, I find it interesting to watch how people change in different situations and it's a credit to them if they stay true to themselves.

Some of my team members were trying to strategize the situation out. "If we help Bullseye do a good job, then regardless of whether they beat us, The Sandbox team still loses three members and we can stay. "Yes, but…."

I know it's a competition. I know this is a game. I know that it's not personal. But I don't like playing dirty. I like to try to do my best and not undermine people. Already the Sandbox was made up of four people whom Joel decided were the weaker

94

members of the two teams (not that they were, I'm just saying that they were the ones previously targeted for elimination). Why would we want to stomp them into the ground?

Yes, I'm sure they planned to come out fighting — working to wow the judges and win. But we all wanted to win so we all had to fight. I like to just try and do the best that I can. That might make me sound passive and a bit Girl Scout, but I can assure you that no one who knows me would call me passive. I'm a red personality through and through. I just don't like punching people in the balls.

Stress and pressure were also starting to get to some contestants. People were getting sharper with each other, and, in trying to be super-focused and super-smart, ended up spinning in circles.

I used to be a waitress, and although some might think it's a silly job. I really learned a lot from it. I waited tables everywhere, from family restaurants to bars to fine-dining restaurants. Let me tell you, I made a ton of money working at the fine-dining restaurant… and I didn't have to work very hard for it. But working at bars and family restaurants, I learned a lot about stress and how to manage it.

Keeping your wits during stressful situation is a very good skill to have. Many a waitress ended up in tears because she was triple sat (three tables at once), five people ordered milkshakes (which we made ourselves and it took tons of time), the kitchen was late with her food, her food was run out before she'd brought out the ketchup, her customers were in a rush, the eggs were overdone, someone at table five wanted more decaf coffee, somebody hadn't put on another pot of decaf, the kitchen screwed up an order…

It's stressful stuff, and if you lose your head, you're a goner. If you let yourself feel at all frazzled, that's it for you. It's all downhill from then on. And you fall fast.

Breathing is so important in keeping yourself calm during stressful situations. In through the nose and out through the mouth, inhaling for five seconds and exhaling for ten. I am not a patient person and have a short attention span and temper… but breathing works for me. Try it.

Perspective is also a great thing to keep. Stress tends to make people over-exaggerate. I actually hate the word "over-exaggerate" because I feel that if you're exaggerating, you're already taking things to extremes, but I feel, in this case, it's a good description. Sound familiar? "Oh my god… my parents are coming at 6:00 for supper. That's only three hours away! My place is so disgusting! I haven't cleaned in ages! I'll never have time to get everything done! They're going to think I live in a pig sty! They're going to think I'm a horrible housekeeper! They're going to think I'm a slob! They'll never want to come over again! They're going to tell everybody how gross my place looks! They won't even want to sit down on my couch! They'll stop loving me!"

Okay, so that last one was a bit much. But you see what I mean. Your mind keeps spinning in circles, "over-exaggerating" all of the outcomes of your unclean place. The real joke is that the whole time you're going over these crazy thoughts in your head… you're not actually cleaning your house. You're getting nothing done!

If, instead of freaking out, you took three deep breaths then said to yourself "Okay, I have three hours until mom and dad show up. I've been a little lax in cleaning so I probably won't have the place spic and span in that amount of time. But, I can pick up all the clutter and hide it in the closet (they won't look there). Then I can wipe down surfaces and vacuum. And if I spray the house up with deodorizer, it will smell like there are absolutely no germs. Plus, no one ever really examines somebody else's house… and, if they do, they deserve to see dirt."

By analyzing the situation and not panicking, you're now able to get done what you need to get done. Without taking years off your life.

As for the challenge itself, knowing real estate turned out to be quite a helpful bit of knowledge to have. Our team did a pretty good job considering we had no direction going into the presentation. Luckily, we had some good speakers who could shovel some good B.S.

Unfortunately for the Sandbox team, they did not win. I have to admit that we breathed sighs of relief at that news. And they ended up in the Judgement Room.

Only Laura emerged unscathed. Debbie, Carly, and Steve had now been permanently eliminated. And, it was announced, there was no more Sandbox. From then on, when you were gone, it would be final.

A few of us had some drinks when we got back to the hotel. High stress, 24/7.

The last note in my journal for Day Three of the competition was "I can't believe it's only day three; it feels like I've been here forever." We were working long days, non-stop. I had no idea what day of the week it was. And now the pressure was mounting — there were only nine of us left.

{ DAY 4 AND MARLON SANDERS }

There are some decisions you make in life because you think they sound good at the time... then, later on, you smack yourself in the head and say "What was I thinking?!"

I seriously hope that is what Joel and Eric now think about Thursday morning's Hacker Safe Immunity Challenge.

I actually think they forgot what show they were producing. Somehow they thought they were putting together an episode of Fear Factor or something.

Anyway, I'm saying it now, I said it then, and the camera captured me... I WAS NOT IMPRESSED.

What the hell am I talking about? I'm sure you must be wondering. Waiting patiently but anxiously to hear...

I won't keep you in suspense much longer.

We arrived on set that morning, ready to hear about our Hacker Safe Immunity Challenge. Yep, we were Pavlov's dogs. We'd learned the drill quickly.

That morning, we were told we would be answering help desk emails. I was excited. I do this! At work, I manage over eighty publishers and I often get phone calls and emails from them or our customers asking for help.

Like I said, I was relieved. If I won the shirt, I wasn't going home. If I wasn't going home, somebody else would be. And that would mean I'd have made it at least one third of the way through. I was psyched.

But then Joel lifted up a cloth that was covering something in the middle of the table. Hidden underneath that cloth was a large clear glass fishbowl half full of LIVE JUICY CANADIAN NIGHTCRAWLERS.

Okay, I am not a bug lover in the least. I can handle mosquitoes and houseflies — and that's about it. I am most scared of cockroaches (they are just so gross). Big juicy worms I am not scared of, they're just yucky (for the lack of a more sophisticated word).

But I was thinking about the task. Thinking about the types of questions I might be asked to answer. Thinking that they were using this bowl of worms as a distraction, a play for the camera. And I wasn't going to fall for it. I was going to remain as cool as a cucumber.

I was, that is, until Joel explained the real reason for the worms' presence.

WE WERE GOING TO EAT THEM!

Yep, Joel wanted us to eat seven-inch long, half-inch wide, browney/purpley, slimy live worms. Did I mention that they were alive and MOVING?

Here's the best part… there were ten help desk emails. We would be allowed a total of fifteen minutes to open, read, and answer them. If we didn't finish all ten, we would be disqualified. BUT, if we ate one worm… we would only have to answer five help desk emails. And if we ate TWO worms, we would only have to answer one.

You have to understand that this challenge was set up so that if you didn't eat the worms, you had no chance to finish. The computers we were using had a slow Internet connection and, even if they didn't, it would be virtually impossible to get all the emails answered properly within that timeframe.

And, really, if you were going to eat one worm, you might as well eat two. What's the big deal?

Joel went around the table asking people whether they wished to come up and eat the worms or whether they chose to answer all of the help desk emails. On the first round, Christine and Charles said that they would not eat the worms (they ate them when asked a second time).

I knew there was no way in hell I was going to be touching those worms, let alone putting them in my mouth.

I was sitting about two-thirds into the group. A bunch of contestants had already gone up and eaten them. Some were being really gross about it, chewing them, opening their mouths to show off their "see-food" (I mean, how old are you, five?). Some were showing off for the cameras, pretending to throw-up, or mixing their hands in the worm bowl for a minute before finally emerging with the worms.

Crazy people!

I decided that I should, at least, get up and pretend I might actually eat one. It always looks good to try to do something. Otherwise, you just look bad. Like I said, I had absolutely no intention of eating a worm. So I stood there and acted.

YES, I ACTED.

Many of the other contestants, as far as I was concerned, were acting too. Just in other ways.

I pretended to struggle with this. I pretended that maybe, just maybe, I would eat them. I pretended to try to grab one out of the bowl.

I was up there a long time. I had people rooting for me to eat them. And probably rooting for me not to.

The whole time I was getting more and more angry at the show. If I was eliminated that day because I didn't win the Immunity shirt, because I didn't eat worms...

How did eating live insects say anything about what kind of businessperson you were? How did it show your Internet marketing skills?

It didn't.

I decided my performance was over, and went back to my chair with the knowledge that, although I would try my best to complete this challenge, I would likely not be immune today.

I was mad... and I had tears of frustration rolling uncontrollably down my cheeks.

Ultimately, I ended up completing seven replies. Not bad, but I was still disqualified.

Everyone else ate their two worms and only had to answer one question in the fifteen minutes — and Alisande won immunity.

I wonder if the others regretted eating those worms when they didn't win?

Joel told me later that he was glad I didn't eat a worm. I guess that's something.

For me, I don't know what they were trying to prove or test, but I think those theatrics were all for dramatic effect. I don't think that challenge had anything at all to do with business, at least in a good way...

In my opinion, there are times in business and in life when people are presented with opportunities to get farther ahead — if they do something they don't want to do. There are always little ways to cheat and worm (pardon the pun) your way out of slimy situations or to get yourself ahead.

Sometimes those options are enticing, sometimes not. But, when those opportunities arise, it's usually easier to get ahead by doing them than not. In fact, sometimes, like in cases like this Immunity Challenge, it might mean that you won't succeed unless you lower yourself and succumb.

Think of a professional athlete and the lure of steroids. Or worse, a lawyer (sorry, I know a lot of lawyers, so I can make fun of them).

But, in all seriousness, opportunities to get ahead by bending your principles come up often and I'm proud to say that I didn't bend. Even if it was something as stupid as not eating worms. And I'm not trying to insult the other contestants here, but I doubt they go around eating worms every day. Everybody could have said no. Then what would the producers have done?

Marlon Sanders was our Classroom teacher that day.

Marlon is a renowned Internet marketer and one of the most respected voices in the industry. Over the last ten years, he has released over thirty educational marketing products. Some of his most popular products are "Amazing Formula That Sells Products Like Crazy" and "Push Button Sales Letters." Marlon is a total marketing ninja — I think he might have been a ninja in a past life. Seriously... Actually I can't picture it, but I'm sure he would have loved to have been a ninja.

Marlon taught us how to create products that win time and time again. He taught us... or tried to teach us... how to be ninjas.

There are three types of businesses to open:

>> Offence

103

» Flanking

» Guerrilla

If you're going to open a business, you will, unless your business is completely "blue ocean" (meaning there's been nothing like it, at all, ever before), open a business that either is offensive, flanking or guerrilla to the leaders.

Rules of business:

1 Leaders expand market share rather than attacking competitors

2 Players two and three attack that leader's weaknesses

3 If you rank fourth, fifth or sixth, you flank

4 Everybody else is a guerrilla

Every business, even successful ones, have strengths and weaknesses. McDonalds was developed because mom-and-pop shops took too long to make the food. I'm sure their burgers were good, but McDonalds saw the weakness of speed and opened shop. Wendy's was created because in order to get speed, McDonalds sacrificed quality. That was their weakness.

Never open a business to compete directly with a strong leader's strengths — attack their weaknesses. That's how you play offence.

To flank another business, avoid direct contact. Wherever they are is where you don't go. Timex, for example, started selling their watches in drug stores. Watches, at that time, were only being sold in department stores.

There are **six basic flanking moves**. These moves are "opposite moves". That means that if they are offering a low price, you offer high price… sounds weird, I know, but read on.

104

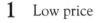

1   Low price

2   High price

3   Small

4   Large

5   Distribution

6   Product forum

Costco is an example of a low price flank. They noticed that products were available in department stores at higher prices and found a way to offer lower prices to their customers by buying in bulk.

Boutique shops flank stores like that of Costco by selling their products at a higher price, making them more exclusive. Also, by having a higher price point, they can afford to offer excellent customer service and status.

In marketing, there are a bunch of weekend seminars that marketers can attend. There are so many that it's very difficult to choose, so the people that put on these seminars have to figure out ways to flank their competition. Sometimes they offer big seminars. Armand Morin actually hosts one called Big Seminar annually. It's huge. Other people host smaller seminars — maybe round-table seminars. More closed off, more exclusive… both are flanking on size.

If you flank based on distribution, you'll have no competition. If you take your product and distribute it where no one else is distributing it — you're flanking. When McDonalds went into Walmart or Starbucks started selling in Chapters/Indigo, they were flanking with distribution.

The whole mp3 music phenomenon is a product form flank. Before mp3s, everyone bought CDs. Now, especially with companies like Apple involved, mp3 music is taking over. And it's all thanks to companies like Napster that flanked the competition.

If you open a guerrilla business, you want to find a market segment small enough that you can defend it.

That means you want to limit the size of your market to:

1   Geographic area

2   Occupation

3   Industry

4   Age or income

5   Special interest

In Canada, maple syrup is a national product and a bit of a cultural institution. Every spring, syrup producers drain the sap from the maple trees and make the syrup — it's a huge event. Then, a company started making maple sugar candies and selling them to tourists coming in to watch the annual event. They were marketing to a geographical area since only the tourists and the residents of that part of the province were offered the product.

There are a lot of magazines and books on the market — and they target different groups. Some magazines, like medical journals, target occupation and industry. There are magazines, like *Teen Vogue*, that target age. And others, like magazines for knitters or those interested in the Civil War, that target special interest groups.

As you can see, there are many ways to launch a guerrilla product. Guerrilla businesses have the highest rate of success, but an important question to ask before getting in too deep is whether your market is large enough to make your millions? Sometimes the markets are so whittled down that, yes, they're very interested, but do they make up enough people to actually make an impact on your business?

Marlon is a very energetic speaker who captured our attention for the entire two hours. I don't know how he does it. I was getting tired just watching. He's like Mick Jagger of The Rolling Stones and Steven Tyler of Aerosmith put together.

Our Execution Challenge was handed out. We had to create a product for a market and talk about how it would be offensive, flanking or guerrilla to other products out there. Then we had to pick which ours would be and how we would market it.

Jason Henderson was our team leader and Laura, with the rest of her Sandbox team eliminated, chose to come back on our team. She'd worked with us before and was comfortable. I was happy she'd chosen us.

All I can say is that our group was a disaster from the get-go. We were totally scattered. We didn't really have a product. We were having problems getting organized. Tasks were being assigned, then people were being pulled away from those tasks...

We finished putting together our Power Point as time ran out. We didn't even have a chance to do any review or practice of the presentation.

What we ultimately decided to create was a new phone... the Tube Phone (my name). The Tube Phone was a phone that could record video and then let you upload it immediately to You Tube. We thought that You Tube could purchase the phone and then sell it as their brand. It would be a flanking move as there are other phones out there that allow the user to upload video to the Internet, but it's a longer process, and you have to pay a monthly fee. Ours would be a lower price (no fee), and it would also be a product that could grow with You Tube.

Unfortunately, we weren't too smart. Charles Trippy was on the Bullseye team, and he was way too in-the-know with video products. And because we only had a couple of hours to work, we were not especially in-the-know. Also, this time, not only would Joel and the judges question us, but the other team was allowed to as well.

So, after our very very puzzling and unorganized presentation, Charles was ready for us. I say puzzling and unorganized because some of our team members didn't even really know what we were talking about and others would have really benefited from practice. Well, everyone can always benefit from practice, but if you don't have the public speaking skills to B.S., you're in B.T., big trouble, with no practice time.

The other team's product was bottled water from Costa Rica in glass bottles instead of plastic. I could have picked a lot of holes in their ideas, but there presentation was way stronger than ours.

We lost the challenge.

And it was time to go back into the Judgement Room.

Lesson learned…don't do something if you don't know what you're talking about. And especially don't do it if you're presenting the idea to someone who has every idea what you're supposed to be talking about.

It was unfortunate that we were so disorganized since Marlon told us afterwards that our Tube Phone was a way better idea than the water. Damn!

Going into the Judgement Room was scary. Only one person was being sent home that night and they were really being eliminated… no more Sandbox. The game was real now.

We all picked Jason Henderson to go home. He was our leader and our team was not led. He picked me and Jason Marshall to go home. I don't know quite how he got that based on our experience…but he and I weren't the closest of friends.

The judges agreed with us, and Jason Henderson went home. I can't say that too many people were surprised or affected. I guess the lesson there is that it's so important to try and connect with people.

The entire competition, Jason had been quite aloof with many of the other contestants. He is very focused on himself and his business, which is great. I respect having an amazing work ethic. But sometimes it went a little overboard. He carried his product around **at all times**. He talked about it at all times. When we all went to the hot tub, he went to the gym.

When you keep yourself apart from the group, the group doesn't care about you one way or another.

When I started working at my government job, I knew it wouldn't be forever. I knew I wasn't a "lifer" (someone who would be there until they retired), and I found it hard to find things in common with the people who were lifers.

But then I found myself without any friends. When I had problems at work, my co-workers didn't really care. When I needed to find certain files, they didn't lift a finger to help. That's when I realized that, even though I wasn't going to be in my situation forever, I needed to be more open and accepting towards them. I needed to at least feign interest in what interested them. Then they, in turn, would consider me and my feelings more. Oh, I know that, ultimately, we are friends of convenience. That, when I'm not at that government job, our friendship will taper off quickly. But the main thing is that I had support and buy-in from people while I was there. And they had me (someone likely to give a different opinion than the others around them).

When we got back to the hotel, I decided that we should have a K.I.S.S. team meeting. We began this competition working so well together and had been getting worse and worse since then. It was time to shape up…or we would all, eventually, be shipped out.

We met over drinks and snacks in the room Laura and I shared and had a very productive meeting. We went over every remaining member's (Laura, Jason Marshall, Alisande and myself) qualities, good and bad. We were pretty frank and we really worked hard to develop a stronger team.

All of us were really proud of ourselves and our accomplishment. We were sure that we would rock-it the next day. Jason joked, "I bet that tomorrow we're split up into new teams." "Don't even say that," was our reply.

Before I went to bed I took two pain medication pills. I had been having bad cramps for much of the day but hadn't wanted to take any medication. I like to avoid it when I can. But I thought it would be better to take some and get a good night's sleep so I would be refreshed in the morning. It was a smart thought....

{ PAIN MEDICATION OVERDOSE }

I had taken three pain medication pills right before Team
K.I.S.S. met and two more afterwards. Five in total. Then I
had a bath to relax my muscles and went to bed, eager to have a
good sleep — to get ready for the next day of competition.

But I couldn't sleep.

As soon as I lay down in bed, I was covered in a layer of sweat.
My body was chilled and I was shaking. My heart started thump-
ing so hard I could feel it through my chest like a hammer.

I started having trouble breathing.

I tried to breathe deeply to relax, but it didn't work. My head
started spinning and I started seeing black.

I didn't know what was happening. I got scared.

Luckily, I used to have allergic reactions to dairy products
and recognized these as the symptoms I would get during an
allergy attack. I knew that I wouldn't die. But I didn't know
where these reactions were coming from since I hadn't had a
problem with dairy in the past year and a half. It had to be a
reaction to the painkillers.

I picked up the phone and tried calling my parents. They're in
the same time zone as Colorado, and they might have been able
to talk me down through the panic to relax my body. I knew that
if I could just get to sleep, my body should be able to recover. I was
nervous, though, because after I would have an allergic reaction,

it used to take me a day or two to get back up to full speed. I didn't have a day or two. I had six hours.

My parents didn't pick up the phone.

So next, I tried calling a good friend of mine in Toronto. I woke him up (it was two hours later in Toronto — making it 4:00 in the morning there). He was amazing and tried to talk me through the attack. It was an extremely hard thing for him to do since I was under strict orders NOT to say anything about the competition. I couldn't talk about whether I was in or out or what I was doing. I didn't talk about how I was feeling because, if it was good, it could mean I was still in; if it was bad, I could be out.

And I couldn't really breathe.

We talked for around forty-five minutes before I got off the phone to try and get some sleep.

I couldn't sleep.

I managed to semi-doze off and on throughout the night. You know, that sleep where you don't feel like you're sleeping but you must be, lightly?

I woke up with my alarm... drenched in sweat. I was shaky. I was WHITE. My heart was still racing.

AND I WAS SCARED.

How was I going to compete? And, if I didn't compete — I was out. I was not going to be out because of something stupid like this. This would not wreck my future.

But I couldn't think about that — I needed help. I crawled out of bed and made my way to Laura's room, hoping she was up.

Luckily, not only was she up, she was getting a makeover. Kaitlyn and Hannah (Eric's sisters-in-law) were over cutting Laura's hair and putting on some make-up.

112

When Kaitlyn saw me, her already very big blue eyes, opened even wider. She rushed right over to me, very worried.

Immediately, she called her mother who called a nurse. Kaitlyn told me to get back into bed, but I knew that I needed to get ready for the show. All I could think about was that I needed to get myself there.

The nurse needed to talk to me so Kaitlyn gave me the phone number. I called her back and gave her my insurance information (thank you Mom for making me buy it). After telling her all about my symptoms, she recommended I go to the Emergency Room. I told her that was not an option (I obviously could not tell her about the show). She told me, quite forcefully, that I had called her for her opinion and her opinion was that I should go to the Emergency Room.

I was not going to the Emergency Room — there was no way. I knew I would not die and that was the only thing that would have sent me to the Emergency Room.

I continued to get ready. The longer I was up and about, the better I felt. Maybe it was just adrenaline, but if I was going out of this competition, Joel Comm was going to have to send me home — I was NOT bowing out.

{ SECTION 3 }

NEAR DEATH

{ NINETY-TWO }
POUNDS

When I was twenty years old, I got very sick. It was around a year after I moved to Calgary.

I had been having a lot of fun, working at a grocery store during the day, hanging out with friends at bars at night. I think I was a pretty typical teenager. I liked to party.

When my family moved back into town, I moved in with them and went back to university. The summer before I went back to school, I had been working at Swiss Chalet, a chicken and ribs restaurant. I ate a lot of French fries throughout the course of my employment there. I don't especially like ribs.

Luckily I have never been the type of person who gains weight easily so it didn't really affect my size, but I didn't feel as toned as I wanted to.

When I quit, I swore off fries.

I'm telling you this not to brag in any way, but to explain why I wasn't concerned with the subsequent weight loss.

While I attended university that fall, I lost weight. I knew I had lost a little bit, but I didn't really think much about it. I wasn't on a diet, but I was walking more and wasn't eating all those French fries anymore. My family hadn't noticed any weight loss. But when my relatives came into town for Christmas, they were shocked at my gaunt appearance. They immediately went to my parents, who were quite upset at their accusations.

We didn't own a scale in my house, so my mom went out and bought one. We had a "family weighing" session. I'm still not sure, to this day, why it was called a family weighing session since really only I had to get on the scale while the others watched.

It read one hundred and two pounds. I had lost about ten pounds and my body fat had sunk lower than that of Olympic gymnasts.

Okay, that probably wasn't too good — but I wasn't sick. I felt fine. And what was wrong with being a bit skinny anyway?

But then, that February, it started. I started having problems breathing. I started having heart palpitations. I started waking up in the middle of the night and was needing to be rushed to the Emergency Room.

Nobody knew what the problem was.

I kept losing weight.

I was accused of being anorexic. I WAS NOT.

The doctors tested me for everything… asthma, tuberculosis, HIV, heart disease (I wore a heart monitor for a twenty-four hour period). They checked my blood counts. They checked for pregnancy. Nothing.

And I was still waking up in the middle of the night needing to be rushed to the Emergency Room.

And my weight was still dropping.

The doctors were stumped. One even tried to convince me that my father had molested me and that I was repressing it… THAT WAS THE FINAL STRAW. I quit going to the doctor.

I finally saw a nutritionist/naturopath named Camille. It was so interesting. Within a two-hour appointment window, Camille had theories on why I was sick.

We did some tests to confirm her suspicions. Because of food allergies, candida (an internal bacteria) had coated my stomach and no food, good or bad, was absorbing into my system. That is why I was losing weight. My body was literally starving itself even though I was eating quite a bit of food.

And because my body wasn't receiving any nourishment, it was shutting down. It was dying.

I weighed ninety-two pounds when I first saw Camille. I shudder to imagine what would have happened if I had stayed with conventional doctors and not looked outside the box for answers. Quite literally, I would be dead. No doubt about it. I showed my childhood friend, Randi, a picture of me from that time and she started crying. She worked in an old-folks home and said that I looked like the old people did right before they died. That really hit me.

Camille put me on a very restricted diet that allowed my body to clear out the bad bacteria and learn how to absorb nutrients again.

From the diet, we learned what foods I was allergic to and which ones I was sensitive to (different neurological responses determine allergy versus sensitivity — but neither are good). I stayed on that diet for a few years, adding in more foods the healthier I got.

And I gained the weight back… which is a very interesting experience in a society that is concerned and obsessed with thin. It plays with your mind a bit.

It was very difficult for me to be trying to gain weight when others were telling me I looked like a model. And I did — size 0 clothes were too big. I always wondered what was smaller than zero. "Should I be wearing 'minus' clothing?" I remember a sales-person getting angry with me for telling her that I wanted to buy

119

pants in a larger size because I was trying to gain weight. "Why would you want to do that!" she huffed. "People would die to look like you!" Yeah, well I almost did. People are so clueless.

Interestingly enough, after my recovery, I learned of many more people with my sort of health problems. And I have since helped a number of people overcome their heath difficulties. So many people aren't knowledgeable about the effects of diet on the body. And why would they be? Doctors don't even know.

My doctor thought I was crazy when I first told her I was seeing a nutritionist. She was still convinced that I must be an anorexic with an abusive parent. Ironically enough, she had horrible arthritis and spent a lot of time in pain.

Since my recovery, that doctor learned more about the connection between diet and health and it has lessened the effects of her arthritis tremendously. Hmmmm…..

I'm actually going to be starting up a health website and using skills I learned from *The Next Internet Millionaire* to market it. So, make sure you check it out. I'll link from my website www.jaimeluchuck.com.

I now think my illness was a gift. I learned so many things about myself and the world from it. I'd almost go as far as to say that I wouldn't trade those lost years… but only almost. I spent the majority of my early twenties sick.

What I learned from my illness is to question. I learned to question everything from the inside out. I learned to be very inquisitive about my thoughts and feelings. I can now very easily recognize what I am feeling and verbalize it. That is a skill, I have learned, that many others do not possess. And it is important.

I learned to question "authority figures". So many people take what doctors tell them at face value.

A good friend of mine was diagnosed with retinitis pigmentosa (RP). RP is a group of inherited eye diseases that affect the retina (the light-sensitive part of the eye). It causes the breakdown of cells in the retina that capture and process light helping us to see. As these cells break down and die, patients experience progressive vision loss. The doctor told him that it was incurable. There was nothing they could do — his only option was to wait and *see* how quickly and how much his vision would deteriorate. And, because of his current vision loss, he had his driver's licence taken away.

Being a friend of mine and knowing my story, he was not interested in waiting to go blind. He did some research and found that Traditional Chinese Medicine (TCM) might help. He began acupuncture treatments that were and are very expensive (and not covered by any benefit plans). He was put on a health diet and was prescribed gunky, smelly Chinese medicinal teas to drink.

Interestingly, but not surprisingly, he has seen tremendous improvement in his eyesight. Although he does not yet have his driver's licence back, his charts have improved so significantly that his eye doctor phoned up his TCM doctor to discuss the findings and has remained in contact with him.

My friend is convinced that he will completely heal his vision. And I believe him.

There are so many examples of people who are let down by "the system" because they believe what they are told, without question. Why have we not been taught to question authority?

Well, I learned that to find answers to questions, it's okay to ask questions. I also learned that it's okay to think outside of the box in other areas of life.

I have a friend who believes that education is the only way to go. "If you don't have a university degree, you'll never be a success." Well, guess what? **She has a degree — I don't. And I make more money at my job than she does at hers.**

She also believes that to further an education, the next step is to get a Master's degree. I think that's a great thing to do. But only do it because you're really interested in the field and want to learn everything about it. Don't do it because you think it's your only option.

My problem with formal education is that it gives you no field experience. You can learn a lot of theories, but until you actually *do* it — what do you really have? A lot of books. That said, I definitely want my doctors and lawyers to have a ton of formal training, but many fields don't need it.

When I want to further my education, I attend seminars from people who have already succeeded at what I want to do. Or, I buy their product if I can't go to the seminar. Or, I get their book out of the library if I can't afford to buy their product.

WHEN I PUT MY KNOWLEDGE FROM *THE NEXT INTERNET MILLIONAIRE* INTO PLACE — I WILL BE MAKING WAY, WAY MORE MONEY THAN MY FRIENDS WHO WENT THROUGH FORMAL EDUCATION… EVERY SINGLE ONE OF THEM.

LIFE LESSON 6: Question, question, question… and then think.

{ SECTION 4 }

COMPETITION CONTINUES

{ MIKE KOENIGS }
DAY 5 AND

All right… it was Day Five and I was sick as a dog. I managed to get myself dressed and in the car. Like I said… if I was going home, it would be because Joel was sending me home in an Execution Challenge.

We arrived at the COMMplex and waited outside, as usual, for the crew to set everything up before we entered.

Nico was amazingly kind. He asked if there was anything he could do to help me. He was so concerned. When I have breathing attacks, the upper-left side of my back becomes very tense during an allergy spell, so I suggested that if he wanted, he could rub my back. He spent the next twenty minutes gently rubbing my back. It helped so much. It got me in the COMMplex.

Then it was time to enter. Time for the Hacker Safe Immunity Challenge.

We were visited by David Hancock of Morgan James Publishing House in New York. They publish a lot of business books for entrepreneurs. Our challenge was to create a book title (minimum of three words), based on words we picked out of a jar. We were allowed to pick ten words, and then could buy more using our e-COMMerce chips. Once we had our title, we were also to write a two-to-three-line subtitle for the book.

I was barely able to sit at the table I was so sick… but I didn't want to let on so I kept sipping at my water, trying not to pass out.

125

I came up with Bare His Skin and it was to be a book about a boy dealing with flesh-eating disease. I was really happy with it, and, after hearing the others, thought I might win. But I didn't — Nico did.

And then he did the most amazing and generous thing…

He stood up and said that he could not accept the Immunity shirt while a friend was feeling so sick.

And he offered me his shirt.

I was shocked! I didn't know what to say. I really wanted to say "yes" since I really didn't think I could finish the day. But this was the safety shirt. Wearing this shirt meant that you wouldn't be going home. How could I take it from him?

I said no.

But he persisted. He was standing there, looking at me with his big caring eyes…and I took it. I took his Hacker Safe Immunity shirt.

I felt rotten — it was a worse feeling than being sick. I felt like such a wimp for taking the shirt. But at the same time, having that shirt took so much stress off my mind that I was actually able to focus on getting better.

I'm still so thankful to Nico. Some of the other contestants were chattering about his motives for giving up the shirt; that he had ulterior motives and it was a strategic move to appear caring to the judges. I choose not to believe nasty people. I truly believe that Nico saved me that day in the competition and I really hope that he would still do the same given the final outcome of the show. It shows a person with real quality.

On our way out of the room, I pulled Nico aside to thank him, but I also told him, "You better not get eliminated tonight or I will never forgive myself." He gave me a long hug.

Then we took a break while Kimberly gave me an essential oil treatment and Kaitlyn brought me some tea. I sat in the massage chair and relaxed. I felt so embarrassed for making such a fuss — but they told me not to think like that.

Joel came over to talk to me. He wanted me to go see a doctor (and he told me that my book title was really good). I told him that I would rather not leave. I really wanted to stay the day and learn. He told me that I could still participate, but that he would prefer that I miss the Classroom lesson and then participate in the challenge. I really didn't want to miss the Classroom — I mean, that's really why I was in Colorado — to learn. I didn't want to miss any opportunities.

I stayed (no disrespect to Joel intended).

Mike Koenigs was our Classroom teacher that day.

Mike's motto is "Breaking the Rules Without Breaking the Law." I like that. For over twenty years, he's turned dreams into reality for Fortune 500 companies, millionaires, billionaires, entrepreneurs, start-ups, authors, musicians, artists, and movie stars. He's worked with huge names. Mike has developed hundreds of websites and dozens of products like Blogging and Podcasting for Authors, How to Make Money on eBay, Internet Infomercial Toolkit, and How to Create, Market & Sell a Product in 24 Hours.

Mike is a video guy.

You Tube is the fourth most popular website behind Yahoo, MSN and Google.

There are over three hundred free video-hosting services online.

Video is number one for entertainment and persuasion.

Portable devices are "it".

127

These are strong statements, but true. People are tuning in to video. People trust video. People enjoy video.

Why use video in your marketing? Because the most popular content online is video. IT SELLS. And, video shows up in search engines.

Video is more effective than the written word and people are tuning in. Right now, video sites are more popular than USA Today, the New York Times and the Washington Post.

And videos work like crazy in niches.

The best thing about video is that no website is required. You can upload it to You Tube, or any other upload site… and go.

Mike taught us that there are six things to know about online video marketing:

1 **Demand** — There should be demand for what you're selling

2 **Quantity** — how many different videos you'll create

3 **Frequency** — how often

4 **Visibility** — where it appears

5 **Affordability** — how expensive they are to create

6 **Repeatability** — it's a numbers game

And the problem with video is that:

» People are afraid

» There is a learning curve

» People think they don't have the looks to be on camera

» They don't know what to say

» It's expensive

128

» It's time consuming

Well, guess what? You can work your way around every single one of those "problems."

I can tell you from being an actor that you don't have to be beautiful to be on camera. In fact, often, unless you're the main character, you don't tend to be stunning. And beautiful people don't tend to be cast as trustworthy. Interestingly enough, there are a lot of actors that work steadily and make a ton of money who would be considered very normal-looking. They are the people that most of us don't recognize on the streets, but, if you know who they are, they pop up in almost every film. They play doctors, lawyers, shop owners, bystanders, scientists, pharmacists.

Even famous actors, before they were famous, might not have been considered beautiful. By being on camera, the public accepted them and their looks until they were "hot". Look at people like Clark Gable — ouch — not what I would consider gorgeous. Nowadays, we have the current James Bond, Daniel Craig (again, not stereotypically handsome — but he has a quality).

It's about that quality on camera, and confidence is excellent for putting across that quality. If you want to be confident on camera, get comfortable in front of it.

Like I said earlier, I basically grew up on camera. We have footage of me dancing on camera, singing on camera, bathing on camera, going to the potty on camera (I know... Mom and Dad, what were you thinking?). But I'll tell you one thing, I'm a natural in front of one (a camera, that is). I'm just used to it.

If you're worried about your looks — don't be. If you're really uncomfortable about looks, talk to someone. You can always get new glasses or contacts. Whiten your teeth with Crest WhiteStrips (I tried the ones sold in my dentist's office and they

DAY 5 AND MIKE KOENIGS

really work). When I worked at the fashion magazine, we Photoshoped the models like crazy. Basically, what people are looking for in an image is clear skin, someone who doesn't look tired (no dark circles), and a nice smile — that's it. And all that can be achieved with make-up (girls and boys). Because, don't kid yourself boys, those men on TV wear make-up — and lots of it.

If you don't know what to say on camera, write it out before-hand and practice it. Don't repeat it word for word, that will likely make it sound stilted, but when you know what you want to say and you're comfortable with the camera — you'll figure it out.

As for learning how to use the camera — that's not too hard. Keep reading…

Here's what you'll need for equipment:

» Webcam or DV Camcorder

» Editing software

» Lights

» Microphones

» Headphones for editing

» Cables, a tripod, and other little necessities

Depending what you want your video for, you can get away with using your Apple computer camera or you can use a camera with a tripod.

Lights are very important. You can use a basic three-point lighting system that works pretty nicely. With a three-point system, you have a back light behind you and two lights in front (each off to one side at forty-five-degree angles from you). You can spend a lot of money on lights or you can spend a little — it really depends on the quality of the video you're shooting and what you're doing. Obviously, if you're setting up a one-shot scenario where you always shoot the same — you'll need less expensive equipment.

I didn't use lights for any of my audition videos. I shot in brightly lit rooms or outside. And I have to say that I was fairly impressed with the lights. So my advice would be to play around a bit before you go out and spend a ton of money.

Microphones are important. If you're shooting in front of your computer, you can either use the internal mic or just buy one, like the Snowball, and plug it into the mic on the computer or camera. If you're moving around, you'll need a lapel mic and you'll want to experiment with those. From my experience, it's hard to find a good lapel mic without spending a chunk of change.

As for editing software, I like Adobe Premier. Final Cut and iMovie are apparently quite good too. I just haven't tried them myself. And iMovie comes with a Mac.

With video, you have about fifteen seconds to catch women's attention; seventeen to twenty-four seconds for men. Good luck — and make it catchy.

Mike created an Infomercial Formula based on A.I.D.A.+A. They are psychological selling techniques.

A: grab **attention**

I: generate **interest**

D: create **desire**

A: get them to take **action**

+

A: **agitate** (squeeze them until they just <u>have</u> to do what you want)

Include an offer in your video. Include a call to action (what your viewers are supposed to do). Make it easy for them to say "Yes — I want to do what you're telling me to do."

There are **twelve kinds of ads**:

1 The **Demo**: showing the product and its features (Here's the Magic Bullet… now let's see what it can do).

2 The **Problem**: show that something is not up-to-snuff in the consumer's life and show a remedy (They have soap scum on their tiles and can't get it off until they use Mr. Clean).

3 The **Exaggerated Problem**: (Plaque on your teeth — the animated germs multiplying until you use Listerine).

4 **Comparison**: (most laundry detergent ads)

5 **Exemplary Story**

6 **Benefit Causes Story**: exaggerate the benefits of the product and show the results (many mortgage ads).

7 **Tell it**: the testimonial (I used Jenny Craig and I lost blah, blah, blah)

8 **Ongoing characters and celebrities**: the Energizer bunny or reoccurring celebrity spokespeople

9 **Exaggeration**: (Women fawning over men who are wearing a certain cologne)

10 **Associated User Imagery**: showing the consumer something that is normally associated with something to prove a point (sunny for happy and bright, etc)

11 **Unique Personality Property**: man on the street interviews

12 **The Parody**

You have to relate to your customers. Ask yourself… what is the problem that keeps my customer awake at night? Who do they trust? And what is the demographic profile? And then, you just have to make your video. No problem, right?

Well, I certainly hoped so, because it was time for our Execution Challenge of the day.

Thankfully, I had really started feeling better throughout Mike's speech. I don't know whether it was the essential oils, the lack of stress due to the Immunity shirt, the fact that the pain medication was getting out of my system, or adrenaline…my guess is it was a mixture of everything.

I certainly felt guilty that, although weak, I was feeling quite a bit better than that morning. I felt like I had robbed Nico of his shirt…but deep down I knew that I wouldn't be better without it.

Unfortunately, before we were given the Challenge, Joel announced that we would be changing up the teams. We were to draw names out of a hat and that would decide the new teams.

I was not impressed. First of all, that meant that our K.I.S.S. team meeting the night before could now be harmful (we discussed everybody's strengths and weaknesses, and had worked to help them overcome those weaknesses). Secondly, I really hoped that I wasn't on Nico's team. If we were on the same team and our team lost — I would have the shirt and he could be sent home.

The teams were chosen:

» Team All-In: *Laura, Nico, Christine and me*

» Team Knuckle-Sandwich: *Charles, Thor, Alisande and Jason*

We had four hours to make a video for Made-Easy Publishing (who, fyi, is the publisher of this book). Made-Easy Publishing is

133

a segment of Morgan James Publishing (who were involved with the morning's Hacker Safe Immunity Challenge).

The video was to represent the hardships of trying to get a book published and how Made-Easy Publishing was a great company for entrepreneurs trying to get their stuff out. I was a bit nervous about the video…we were up against the "You Tube King."

I kept getting sharp pains in my stomach throughout those four hours we worked on the project, but I was really proud of myself for giving it everything that I had.

We decided, based on Joel's response to our graphic design on Day Two, to play it safe. We also knew that Charles's team would not (and that hurt us with our graphic — not being corporate enough).

We put together a quality video, it was very informercial-like but it had all the elements. As a team, though, we didn't work together very well. Some of our members weren't very happy to be on our team. They liked the comfort of their former team-mates. It was unfortunate, because I believe you have to be adaptable in business — and we had enough elements to be successful — I just don't know if they were put to the best use.

Like I said, our video was good. Knuckle-Sandwich's video was funny. Very You Tube, *quelle* surprise. It was funny, but I don't think it really marketed the company. However, our team weren't the judges…and we lost.

It was off to the Judgement Room again. Laura had been in that room every night except the first — she made a lot of jokes about that to Joel and the cameramen.

In the Judgement Room, we all picked Christine to go, except Christine who, if I remember rightly, picked Nico. They sort of had a non-liking issue between them.

She was crushed and I felt badly for her. I tried to reassure her in the car on the way back to the hotel, as her closer friends (her former team members) had won dinner out with Joel and Mike and so were not with us.

I think I mentioned this before, but I find the study of people and the way they act in different situations to be very interesting. The way people can change on a dime when the circumstances change never fails to surprise me. Ever.

DAY 6 AND
{ BRAD FALLON }

O kay — here's my biggest beef with the NIM production. They gave us absolutely no warning about anything. I don't mean they should have told us exactly what we were going to be doing. But certain hints might have been nice like… "Hey guys, dress to be outside and walking around on Saturday." Yeah, I'm thinking that would have been nice.

Instead, they kept all their plans to themselves. So, I wore a blue wool suit and heels that day.

When we arrived at the COMMplex, we found out that we would be heading outside for the Hacker Safe Immunity Challenge.

Then we drove to a children's race where we were going to be selling popsicles. WALKING AROUND SELLING POPSICLES. That sucked.

It was so hot, and I was already sweating to death in my suit. I had a decision to make, I could take my jacket off and just wear the little tank top I had on underneath — but since we hadn't been given any warning that we would be outside… I didn't have any sunscreen on. I have very British skin. It burns — and fast.

I went with the burnt skin choice and left the jacket in the van.

We had twenty popsicles to sell and we could ask any price we wanted. The person with the most money earned, would be the challenge winner. We would have twenty minutes, but, because it was so bloody hot, if we didn't sell our popsicles quickly, they would melt anyway.

On your mark, get set... GO.

And we were off. There were only seven of us left, but that meant that there were one hundred and forty popsicles between us. That's quite a lot with which to saturate a not-so-huge market. And it saturated quickly. All of a sudden, kids everywhere seemed to have popsicles in hand. I think there was someone else selling them too.

It was an interesting challenge trying to sell these treats. Since we had no price, we could ask for any amount. But we couldn't tell people what we were selling them for... and we couldn't lie. Also, we couldn't tell people we were going to donate the money to a charity, even if that wasn't a lie (because we had to hand in the money and couldn't spend any of our own).

Also, we each had a cameraman following us so we definitely stood out and generated interest. But most people don't like being on camera, they get nervous, so we weren't always a welcomed presence.

Being friendly and smiling was a good thing. Unfortunately, I do my best around guys... not moms. Moms are not my best market. I don't have kids nor do I look like I have kids. And I was wearing a business suit and heels at a race on a Saturday. Not fitting in, that's for sure. I stuck out like a sore thumb. And it's cold-calling — I hate that (if I haven't said that one hundred times already).

As much as I really didn't enjoy that challenge, I did okay. I managed to sell a few of my popsicles and earned $20.50. I gave a bunch away at the end, just so they wouldn't go to waste. My camera guy got my very last one. He deserved it, lugging around that heavy camera, running after me. It was pretty funny. At one point, some little five-year-old thief ran up to me and stole one of my popsicles. Who raises these children?

Unfortunately, my $20.50 put me in second place behind Nico, who sold quite a bit. I can't remember what the actual dollar amount was but he certainly had a way with selling. I committed this fact to memory. Laura came third. Way to go Team All-In! Unfortunately, however, this wasn't the Execution Challenge. It was the Immunity Challenge and Nico was now immune for the day. That meant, if we lost, that either Laura or I would be gone. I tried to think positive thoughts for All-In.

Brad Fallon was our Classroom speaker that day.

Brad began his business, My Wedding Favors (.com), with a $2,000 start-up investment in 2004. It earned $1.2 million in first-year revenue, $7.8 million in 2005, and $32 million in 2006. Apparently a ton of people buy wedding favours. Weddings are big business. He is the author of Creating Customers Out of Thin Air: Secrets of Online Marketing for Offline Businesses and the host of Search Engine Radio. Brad also co-founded StomperNet (the leading subscription-based Internet marketing training program). Very cool. He was also in the pilot episode, albeit very briefly, of Beverly Hills, 90210.

Our Classroom time was spent talking about how to build your e-business faster. How to get more money faster.

> *"People tend to overestimate what can be done in a year and underestimate what can be done in five."*
>
> ~Lick

Ideas mean little...execution is everything. That is so true. I mean, you need ideas. But you can have all the ideas in the world, and if you're not executing them, so bloody what?

If you understand your customers, everything is better.

And always be thinking "what's next?" now.

When you're in business, you want to be equally good at **strategy** and **execution**. Unfortunately, it's very rare for people to be good at both. That's why it's a good idea to look for a partner who is good at whatever point is your weakness.

As a CEO of a company, your job is to:

» Articulate the vision

» Drive the culture

» Hire good managers

"If you have everything under control, you're not moving fast enough."

~~ Mario Andretti

That is also very true. They say that most people aren't really qualified to be in their jobs. They move up and up, until they get to a position where they're not good enough to move up. I don't really think that's true. I think that people get comfortable in a job that's too easy. And they stay in that job because why bother doing something harder? Actually, not that I really think about it... there are both types of people in this world.

Brad also spoke to us about what attracts people when they are looking at a website design. "What do people focus on?" is an important question to ask yourself because you want to lessen your bounce rate (the number of people who go to your home page and leave without exploring your site).

People look at human faces. They read captions. They read headlines, *p.s.* notes, and blue underlined links. So layout and design are really important. What you put on your site can really make the difference.

What that ultimately means is that you have to test and test… and then test some more. Just putting up a site is, ultimately, not enough. You could be losing out on tons of money and you wouldn't even know it.

Even if you have a professional designer doing your site, they might not know the best design layout for your customers. What if you tried a different picture? A different headline? Different colors?

How do your sales differ over the course of time?

Make sure you chart out your successes. Charts are amazing descriptions and motivators. Charts and graphs. Visually seeing results is a fabulous tool.

Whatever you do, keep working. Don't start over. Many people make the mistake of deciding to start over when maybe they just need to tweak and test. Maybe they need to redesign or maybe they need to refocus, but trashing the product only means that you wasted both time and money.

I had hoped Brad would talk more in depth about StomperNet and building successful websites. Unfortunately for me, he talked mostly about general business. It was still very interesting though. And he is obviously a very successful man. So he knows what he's talking about.

It was also unfortunate that our Execution Challenge did not coincide with what Brad was talking about (not that this was his fault). Our Execution Challenge had to do with eBay.

We had to go out to a garage sale and buy something to sell on eBay. Our budget was $20. (Again, I'm going to add my side note of "Hello, wearing a wool suit and heels today!!!")

We drove out to the garage sales. Now, anyone who knows me can tell you that I am not a junk collector. In fact, I usually get rid

141

of things way too soon and end up needing them again later. So I have no clue about junk. I collect nothing. I have never collected anything (except a bunch of My Little Ponies when I was nine — but they were just to play with).

I also have never bought anything off of nor even really looked at eBay. The only thing I really knew about eBay is what I learned from that Weird Al song. Really, I was starting to think I was kind of pathetic with all that I did not know with regard to these challenges.

If you haven't heard the Weird Al Yankovic song, it's great. And it teaches you a lot about eBay. You gotta love the media. In fact, below are the lyrics... you'll laugh and laugh. It's to the tune of some Backstreet Boys song (I Want It That Way). Weird Al rocks!

The "eBay song"

A used ... pink bathrobe

A rare ... mint snowglobe

A Smurf ... TV tray

I bought on eBay

My house ... is filled with this crap

Shows up in bubble wrap

Most every day

What I bought on eBay

Tell me why (I need another pet rock)

Tell me why (I got that Alf alarm clock)

Tell me why (I bid on Shatner's old toupee)

They had it on eBay

I'll buy ... your knick-knack

Just check ... my feedback

"A++!" they all say

They love me on eBay

Gonna buy (a slightly-damaged golf bag)

Gonna buy (some Beanie Babies, new with tag)

(From some guy) I've never met in Norway

Found him on eBay

I am the type who is liable to snipe you

With two seconds left to go, whoa

Got Paypal or Visa, what ever'll please

As long as I've got the dough

I'll buy ... your tchotchkes

Sell me ... your watch, please

I'll buy (I'll buy, I'll buy, I'll buy ...)

I'm highest bidder now

(Junk keeps arriving in the mail)

(From that worldwide garage sale) (Dukes Of Hazzard ashtray)

(Hey! A Dukes Of Hazzard ashtray)

Oh yeah ... (I bought it on eBay)

Wanna buy (a PacMan Fever lunchbox)

Wanna buy (a case of vintage tube socks)

Wanna buy (a Kleenex used by Dr. Dre, Dr. Dre)

(Found it on eBay)

143

Wanna buy (that Farrah Fawcett poster)

(Pez dispensers and a toaster)

(Don't know why ... the kind of stuff you'd throw away)

(I'll buy on eBay)

What I bought on eBay-y-y-y-y-y-y-y-y-y.......

Have you stopped laughing yet? That song is just so funny.

Anyway, we had to buy some junk at this garage sale. Then we would bring it back to the COMMplex where we would have three hours to post it up on eBay. After that we'd wait...

The bidding would take place over twenty-four hours. That meant we were all safe until Monday morning as we had Sunday off. I can't tell you how relieved Laura and I were.

Nobody ever *wants* to go home. But on Saturday night... We (Laura and I) wanted to go out, have some fun, and blow off some steam. We didn't want to be stuck with one of us having to pack and leave (everyone who was eliminated had to leave the hotel — we didn't know where they were going but it turned out to be a gorgeous ranch house up in the mountains... it almost made me wish I'd been kicked off when I heard that — almost).

We bought packaged NFL, NBA, NHL, and MLB sports figurines. I had no idea what they were worth, but I'd heard that people buy packaged stuff — you always see that in movies, where some geek has a bunch of packaged toys (no offence to those of you who collect that stuff). So that's what we bought. We had something like sixteen of them. We also had some junky plaque of a football player, a golf club and a bunch of Donald Duck mugs.

The other team bought a bunch of Coca-Cola memorabilia crap. They won. Who knew?

144

But, since we didn't know at the time who was going to ultimately win, we were able to go out on that Saturday night and let loose.

LIFE LESSON 7: Get out and have a good time.

You can't work all the time. It's not healthy. And we had been in the COMMplex for six very long days. Stressed all the time. Constantly working. We needed the break.

We went to a bar...

And when the bar closed, we went back to the hot tub...

Hey, what can I say? Internet marketers (or even potential ones) know how to have a good time.

A NOTE ON
{ CAMERAS }

I was hating cameras! Remember when I told you that I was comfortable with them? Well, I learned that I have a maximum tolerance level.

I felt like Angelina Jolie, that everywhere I went, the cameras were there. Watching. Whenever I talked to someone, there they were. Whatever I was doing, there they were. It really made me glad that I was not famous — it might have been the first time ever that I had felt that way.

Even when the cameras were not on us, I felt like everything I said was being judged and thought over to see if it could be used against me in the confessionals. Whatever we said could be used against us if the NIM folks wanted dirt. Not a good situation — especially if people are just trying to relax and have fun.

No offense to the NIM crowd — but I really began to understand how and why celebrities punch out the paparazzi. Luckily, I think the cameramen ended up drunker than we did that night, so nothing was brought up the following day.

147

{ KRIS JONES }

L aura and had a great time together on Sunday. By Sunday night, we knew that one of us would be eliminated. But she and I were okay.

That meant a lot to me because many of the other contestants wouldn't have been so good about it. They would have been looking at me and seeing direct competition — but not Laura. She was able to let it go so we could have fun. I was glad that I could let it go too. We went shopping, out for dinner, and had Nico take pictures of us — we had a blast.

That Monday morning, we were dressed and ready to go face the music of our pathetic eBay sale attempt.

The Judgement Room was awful. The three of us had worked well as a team, we just made a bad decision on our product and really knew nothing about how eBay worked. What can you say to that?

Joel asked Nico to select who he would pick out of me and Laura to do a JV with? I felt really badly for Nico being put in that situation. He hemmed and hawed for a while — I don't really know if he ever gave a definite answer. He pointed out strengths and weaknesses for both of us. Very politically correct — but what a situation to be put into.

Then Joel asked us (Laura and I) each to defend ourselves and why we should be kept in. Again, I thank my presentation skills — they probably saved me right then and there. I was able to come up with quick, on the spot, semi-good-sounding reasons why I would be the best person to continue in the competition. My thoughts were relatively structured and I hammered home my points.

We were all three holding hands when the judges came back into the room. They picked Laura to go home. I let out a deep breath. I never really thought it would be me — but it really sucked that it was Laura. Part of me was hoping that it was going to be neither of us. I know, I know — impossible, but hey...

I was so glad that was over.

What surprised me most was what came next. I haven't talked much about our e-COMMerce chips throughout this book, but we used them almost every day to buy into activities, or buy up on challenges (like more time or more options on eBay). But, as contestants were eliminated, they were asked who they would like the remainder of their chips to go to. They had the option of picking a particular person or splitting them up between two or more people.

Laura gave all of hers to Nico — I was never sure why. Maybe she owed him some from an earlier challenge? I have to admit, I felt a bit hurt. I had thought we were friends.

And now I was sharing my hotel room only with Alisande. She had moved in after Christine was eliminated. It was just the two Canadian girls left! No offense to Alisande, but the room was definitely going to have a different vibe.

I think the NIM producers had learned from the popsicle day. For this next Hacker Safe Immunity Challenge, we were taken back to the hotel to change into workout clothes and runners. It was going to be an outside day... and we were given sunscreen — go NIM team!

We drove up into the Colorado Rocky Mountains. I love the mountains. They're so beautiful and peaceful. As much as I love the city, when I get immersed in nature, my stress just melts away. When I lived in Calgary, I could see the Canadian Rockies from higher points in the city. The mountains, and Banff, were only about an hour away.

The plan was to do a hike through the mountains to test our endurance. It was an extremely hot day outside and I hadn't eaten breakfast. I was seriously hoping this wasn't an extreme endurance test. I was picturing an eight-hour hike up the mountainside, with some strenuous rock-climbing... contestants dropping off like flies until only one of us was left standing.

But this was nothing of that sort... we hiked for about twenty minutes. The scenery was gorgeous. When we got to a rock shack somewhere up the mountain, we all had to line up. I was wondering if now there would be some outrageous challenge like "You'll have to find your way back to Loveland," or something...you never know. After the worm fiasco, I was prepared for anything from the producers.

But then Joel announced that, today, all of us were immune! We were all presented with Hacker Safe Immunity t-shirts.

It was really great to know that we were all safe. Everybody relaxed a notch. It was noticeable. We were ready to have fun.

And fun we were going to have.

Our Classroom speaker for the day was Kris Jones.

Kris is considered one of the leading Internet marketing experts in the world. His company, Pepperjam, is recognized as a 2006 *Inc. 500* Company (number 293), an honor that is given to the top 500 fastest growing privately held businesses in the United States by *Inc. Magazine*. Pepperjam works with many really well-known companies such as Old Spice, Nordstrom, Sesame Street and JLo.

151

Today, we focused on fun. At Pepperjam, Kris is adamant that his employees have a good time. In fact, their workplace is filled with toys and games.

You would think that if employees were having fun, that they would not really produce. But Kris finds it's just the opposite. If people are having fun and enjoy being at work, ultimately they will work better… and be more creative doing it.

I would have to say that I agree with him.

Experts say that the best way to stimulate creativity and energy is to get your blood flowing. Most people think that if they work out, they'll be tired. But, really, that's not the case (although it's the excuse I like to give for not working out). In reality, because your body's moving, you get more done and ultimately make up the time you've spent working out, and more. I have to caution, though, that the high energy results don't happen immediately. Usually, whenever I can convince myself to exercise, my body is so out of shape and I push myself so hard, that I am physically exhausted to the point of pain. But, if you continue through that, the results are supposed to be amazing.

We played games the rest of the day. Because All-In was two players short of Knuckle-Sandwich, we were allowed to steal a player from them. I really wanted to take Charles, but Nico wasn't so sure. He thought that perhaps we should take a weaker player (why take Joel's favorite was his rationale). I really didn't agree. If, let's say, Charles was "Joel's Golden-Boy," wouldn't it stand to reason that our team might then begin to win? And, if we won, we wouldn't be in the Judgement Room where one of us would be eliminated.

"Fine," he said, "But know that if we lose… it will either be you or me that goes home. Joel's not going to get rid of Trippy." I was prepared to deal with that. I was also not convinced that

Charles was a shoe-in. I hadn't worked with him yet and was hoping to have the chance during the course of this competition.

Charles came to All-In and the games began. We played team ping pong, Foosball, Nintendo Wii Tennis, and Jeopardy. I had so much fun and it was a great bonding experience. Plus, now I really want to buy a Wii. It's too bad I need to save up enough money to buy a house with a bigger living room before I can use it. My living room barely has enough room to walk around the furniture.

That night we all went out for dinner at a really good Mongolian grill place. I ate two plates of nice and spicy rice noodles. I love spice and, like I said earlier, I never knew what we were going to eat. We ate a lot of sandwiches (bread is one of my "sensitivity" foods — I really shouldn't eat it).

While we were standing at the grill, Joel asked me about my JV ideas. I blanked. I had nothing to tell him. I felt like a real moron.

Honestly, I had been so focused on the daily challenges, learning, and trying to stay in the competition that I had given absolutely zero thought to any type of joint venture idea.

It really made me stop and think. When you're so busy working and working... non-stop working, you can never create and build. You're just maintaining. With business, you have to do both. Obviously, you have to maintain. But you also have to stop, breathe... and figure out how you can grow.

My brother, Ryan, is a musician (I talked a bit about him earlier with the musical audition video). He recently opened up a singing studio. He had been studying Speech Level Singing with a teacher in Los Angeles for many years and decided to open up a Toronto outlet. He started advertising and had a website built. And he started getting students. He was ecstatic. He was making money. He felt successful.

When he wasn't teaching, he was working on different ways to market his business in order to get more clients. And when he wasn't doing that, he was figuring out business strategies to help him get more dedicated, long-term students (who would actually show up for the lessons).

But then his client list grew. He started being busy with the teaching part of his business all day, every day. Which was great, don't get me wrong. He was happy. Busy, happy — and raking in the money.

And then he realized that he didn't have any time left to figure out new business plans. He was spending all of his time on maintenance — none on development. He had to decide to make the sacrifice of less money coming in (less clients), in order to have more strategy time. It's a hard decision to make and, if he could afford to, he would, and should, spend even more time on the development side.

He could:

» get a partner to run that end of the business

» train another instructor to ease his workload so he can focus on development

» outsource projects so he can try to do everything

But, as Ryan is finding out, in businesses where your time is your commodity, there is only so high you can go before you're at your ceiling. To break through that ceiling, you have to find a way to distribute yourself to a larger crowd. That could be through large seminars, DVDs, books, and any other means of communication.

LIFE LESSON 8: Make time for business development.

154

I think they say that luck is the outcome of opportunity and preparation. You often hear, in show business, of people getting "lucky breaks." And it's true that some people get picked out of a crowd and soar to success while others try and try and try with no results. But, I'm sure there are many people who get the "Hey, you… yeah, you in the crowd. Read this line for me and we'll see what you got." If they have no skill or talent, they get pushed right back into the crowd. It's just that nobody ever hears of those stories.

A friend of mine back in Regina once had the opportunity to audition for a film starring Matthew Fox (back then, he was only known from *Party of Five*). She was not an actor and had no interest to be one, but she certainly took the opportunity to audition. I was so jealous and mad. How come she got the chance to audition? I would have loved to — given anything to have that chance (I didn't live in Regina anymore). Now, she didn't get the part because, she's right, she's not an actor. If she had the talent, maybe now she'd be on Lost or something too.

> **LIFE LESSON 9: Always be prepared to answer questions about your plans. You never know when an opportunity will strike.**

{ MIKE FILSAIME }

D ay Eight started off on a very interesting note. Some contestants were starting to panic. The teams were small now, three on each. And everybody left was pretty strong. The losing team would be almost "Eenie-Meenie-Minee-Mo" in the Judgement Room. Fear was in the air.

Thor approached me with an offer. "If I win the Immunity shirt and my team wins the Execution Challenge, then I'll give the shirt to you — and if you win the shirt and your team wins the challenge, then you'll give it to me," was his proposal.

It seemed a bit sketchy. I asked for some time to think it over. I also asked if this was allowed. He checked with Eric and it was.

I felt really weird about the deal but I kept thinking... if he doesn't do this deal with me, he'll approach someone else, and I would hate to be on the losing end of that stick. Also, if he's making this kind of deal, I wondered, who else was strategizing with each other?

So I reluctantly agreed — knowing that I now had a 33 percent chance of immunity.

Our Hacker Safe Immunity Challenge was a research competition. Boy, I was glad I had made that deal. I have never considered myself good at researching. I just get too bored with it (maybe I'm ADD — maybe I'm just a red personality.)

We were each at our laptops. Joel would give us something to look up. It might be finding a web page with the information. It might be finding an image. It might be finding the exact answer. Whatever we needed to find, we had to Instant Messenger (IM) it to Joel. The last one in would have to pay out e-COMMerce chips to stay in the game.

Research is an important skill to have when you're doing business. You need it to do basically anything. Knowing how to use research tools is definitely an asset. I learned very quickly that having a quick Internet connection is also an asset.

I didn't have that. My Internet was painstakingly slow and I would sometimes ring in last because of it. Eventually it just stopped working altogether and, luckily, Joel let me use another contestant's computer (who was already out.)

That made a huge difference. I learned that I'm actually pretty quick at researching facts. What I found more interesting than the research was watching the dynamics in the room. Who was competing with whom? I mean, in reality, we were all competition with each other. But some people had ideas of who their "real" competition was.

Nico, for example, used up all of his chips, because he was fighting desperately to beat me. He considered me his only competition — seeing Charles as someone who was in no way going to be eliminated.

Thor wanted to be the last one standing on his team… and he wanted to beat Nico. But, he didn't care if he beat me since we had our agreement.

I just wanted to win. a) because I had never won a Hacker Safe Immunity Challenge on my own (though I had worn the shirt twice)… and b) because I wasn't especially proud of my agreement with Thor. I wanted to earn immunity — I had been so close so many times.

Nico eventually ran out of chips, so he was out. Now, all the contestants were out except ironically, me and Thor.

I don't know what Thor's plans were, but I planned to keep playing. I was strong in this challenge. But Joel called "last round." We had been playing for what seemed like ages. I don't really know how long it was, but it must have been 1 hour or 1 ? hours.

I took the round — and WON THE HACKER SAFE IMMU- NITY SHIRT. Yeah for me! And, may I say... FINALLY!

An FYI (for your information) to people not familiar with search engine research, here are some tips:

» Be specific with what you're searching

» Put words that are supposed to be together in quotation marks

» Add subjects together with the "plus" sign

For example... if I wanted to find out how much a Nintendo Wii costs, this is what I would Google-search:

"Nintendo wii" + price

If I wanted to find out which years the Edmonton Oilers won the Stanley Cup with Wayne Gretzky, I would look up:

"Edmonton Oilers" + "Stanley Cup" + "Wayne Gretzky"

... and then I might need to add years into that equation.

Do you see what I mean?

Google also has an "images" tab where you can choose to search images. You can look up "maps." You can seriously look up anything on Google, and you can find anything on the Internet if you know how to look

Our classroom speaker that day was Mike Filsaime.

Mike is an author, software developer, renowned speaker, personal coach, business consultant, and an intensive marketer. He really knows how to teach people in a way that "sticks" — I was looking forward to that. In 2006, his company, MikeFilsaime.com, Inc., did nearly $4.5 million dollars in sales.

On this day, Mike was here to talk to us about viral marketing, a.k.a. "word of mouth marketing on STEROIDS."

Here's something to note… on average, people decide to buy the seventh time they visit a site. What this means is you should definitely get their name and email address the first time they arrive. You'll need to keep chipping away at them.

People don't like to give away their personal information, so you might have to offer them an incentive in order to get it. I know — giving away stuff for free sucks. But, think about it. Ultimately, you'll be ahead of the game. Use viral marketing to create attention.

These days, there are so many delivery mechanisms through which to market your message. There is:

» Internet

» Email

» Instant messaging

» Cell/mobile phones

» SMS text messaging

» You Tube

» Social networks (MySpace, Facebook, etc)

The first thing you need to ask yourself is… "Is my messaging, product or service WORTH TALKING ABOUT?"

Let's hope so. If yes, you need to create BUZZ.

You can **create buzz** a number of ways. Mike talks about twelve:

1 new

2 fresh

3 inspirational

4 innovative

5 controversial

6 edgy

7 humorous

8 heartwarming

9 taboo

10 secretive

11 engaging (participation)

12 suspenseful

When Google first released their g-mail, they used *new, innovative, secretive, engaging* and *suspense* buzz techniques to get attention. And they spent no money achieving their buzz.

They played with scarcity by allowing only a certain number of g-mail accounts. People actually bid to get these email accounts on eBay, they were so popular. There was huge demand created by this limited supply.

The key to viral marketing is that you want people to view your message and then pass it along. Online, adding the "share with a friend" feature is tremendously helpful. But still, people are going to ask: "What's in it for me?" If you have an answer to that question, your message will spread faster (if they like your answer, that is). So make sure you think of an answer.

Another way to promote wildfire spread of your message is to get an authority figure to pitch your product. Again, unless you know an authority figure, you might have to figure out an answer to their "What's in it for me?" question. Everybody needs an answer to that question in business.

The **Infection Stage** of your viral marketing is crucial. This might sound horrible, but you want your message to spread like the plague. If you think about it in terms of medical infections, there are different ways to spread disease:

» airborne

» indirect contact (germs on railings, etc)

» person-to-person contact (two people have to touch)

» intimate contact (saliva)

» sexual contact (well, I think you know...)

Obviously, to best spread your message, you need to spread your message through the air. Everybody needs to breathe it in. You don't want to have to wait for that other stuff to happen — skip the foreplay. Infect everybody.

A massive initial infecting stage will have the greatest effect in most cases. Have a huge media blitz, a massive JV launch, etc.

Then, best case scenario, you want to have a **Tipping Point**. Tipping points happen when **Mavens** (like Oprah) and/or **Super Connectors** (like bloggers) continue to spread your word.

And then you work to keep people talking: press releases, articles, videos, forum posts, blogs, etc.

162

Your goal... TOTAL MARKET SATURATION.

The key to long-term duration in a market is to have a post-launch strategy.

Viral marketing is a very interesting subject. You never know what is going to catch on with people. Some of the stupidest things become super popular. For instance, there's this ugly guy who sings badly — and his videos have been seen by millions! Now he has his own website and sells merchandise. But unfortunately, there's no formula to what people latch on to. If I put up a video of my singing, I doubt it would go viral (and I seriously doubt I would want it to.)

My suggestion would be to keep trying and testing different styles and methods. If one message doesn't work — try another way to get buzz. Sometimes you can be too edgy and your message is lost. Sometimes you're going for funny, but you misread your target market and they don't find the humor in it. Just tweak and go again. Don't give up.

Mike (just like every other guru who taught us at NIM) has a huge DVD set that goes way more in depth than the two-hour session he did with us. I plan to get copies of every set from these guys... and I highly recommend that you guys look into them too. Please see the back of the book or go to my website (www.JaimeLuchuck.com) for more information.

Joel came back into the Classroom and we were given our Execution Challenge.

The Instant Buzz toolbar is one of Mike's products. It's a free downloadable toolbar that sits in your Internet browser. As users surf the 'Net, different ads appear on the bar. Our challenge was to take the Instant Buzz toolbar, make some changes to it, and present a new marketing strategy.

That doesn't sound too difficult, does it? Let me tell you a little secret. It's very hard to be critical of other people's products when they're sitting in front of you and are being your judge. That's something we had to deal with at times during this competition. We might have been asked to offer suggestions for our gurus' products, but that might have just been for the competition, not because they were unsatisfied with their products. And nobody likes hearing that their product is "ugly" or "sucks.". You have to somehow find tactical ways to say that and get your plans to improve their product across without offending them. Not easy, that's for sure.

Team All-In (Nico, Charles, and me) fit together well. We used all of our strengths to put together a new toolbar. We worked well given the time restraints and even had time to rehearse our presentation, not something Team K.I.S.S. every really had time to do. We were pretty confident with our product.

But both teams put together good presentations and, unfortunately for All-In, although some of Knuckle-Sandwich's suggestions were not exactly technically do-able, the judges didn't question them. I guess they were looking more for presentation than technically correct strategies. This is where we fell.

Oddly enough, there was a member of each team who did not do well in the presentation part of the challenge, Nico from our team and Alisande from Knuckle-Sandwich.

I'm not sure why, but Alisande didn't talk during their presentation. She turned the Power Point slides. Both Thor and Jason are very good speakers (as I have previously mentioned) and they might have been concerned with their team putting the best face forward and, therefore, wanted their best speakers talking... I don't know.

It was strange because in past Knuckle-Sandwich and Bullseye presentations, Thor did all the talking. It was a different strategy than my teams ever took. Other than the presentation where only the team lead (and that was me) was allowed to talk, all of my team members spoke. I wonder if it was Thor's decision to be the only one speaking or if it was a team decision everytime?

Nico was not strong in our presentation, which was surprising since he's not a bad presenter. But, after the Hacker Safe Immunity Challenge had been awarded to me, it almost seemed like he gave up, like he knew he was out. It was like the wind had been taken out of his sails. Unfortunately, I was the last person who could have helped him out of this mood since he considered me his direct competition — and might have blamed me for calling Charles over to our team, I don't know.

The judges asked that both Nico and Alisande go back onto the stage. They were both asked to give a 30 second critique of the other team's presentation. Alisande stumbled at first, but eventually came to life about 20 seconds into her time. Nico never really did.

We lost.

And it was back to the Judgement Room **again**.

I was really beginning to hate that room. Granted, I knew that this time I was immune, but I wanted nothing to do with that room — ever again — no matter which contestant I was in there with. I wanted to start winning for God's sake!

The judges were harsh to the point of comical in the Judgement Room and I had to work hard to contain my amusement. I don't think that would have gone over well. They were being very critical of both Nico and Charles. Nico, they said, had had a defeatist attitude ever since he lost the Immunity Challenge earlier that day. Charles, they feared, was a "one-trick pony" (their words, not mine). It went back and forth. Back and forth. Nico, Charles. Charles, Nico.

165

Eventually, I was asked who I thought should go home between the two of them. This was a difficult decision to make (well, not a difficult decision, because I knew what I was going to say, but it was difficult for me to say out loud).

Nico had done so much for me earlier on in the competition. Without him, I might not have still been in the game. He'd been a great support. And we'd become friends. But, ultimately, I hadn't been impressed with his attitude that day... I picked him to go home.

So did the judges.

I felt like a traitor, like I should have stuck my neck out to help a friend — one who could have potentially given up so much for me. I didn't know Charles. I had never worked with him. He seemed like a really genuine guy but we hadn't really hung out. We weren't what I would call friends.

Both Nico and Charles are very smart people. And I don't think people can understand, unless they've been in a similar situation, how it feels to be put under the gun to critique and choose between people. It's not easy... and it's not fun.

In a way, though, I was glad that we didn't win that challenge. Winning would have meant going over to Joel's house for "movie night" and I really just wanted to get back to the hotel.

I really needed to talk to people who were on my side, who weren't fake. Even though I couldn't tell my family anything, not who I was around, not what I was doing, or anything I had done or had felt since the Sunday before, I really just needed to hear some genuinely friendly voices.

Like I said, Thor's proposal that morning had thrown me quite a bit. I hated thinking that everybody was conspiring behind everyone else's back. I hated thinking that somebody could be making deals that might get me eliminated. I hated thinking that maybe people were specifically trying to get me off the show — hey, it happened to some contestants. I won't say how, just that I saw it happening. I really wished that people would play the game straight up.

But it *was* a game — and I had to remember that.

I can't stress how important it is when playing any game (including the game of life), that you not give up. Talking with Mike Filsaime after the Judgement Room, I found out that our team lost because of Nico's 30-second speech test. If he had performed better than Alisande, we three would still be All-In and either Thor (well, I guess not Thor because of our deal), so either Alisande or Jason would have been gone.

LIFE LESSON 10: Don't ever give up. Ever. Fight to the death.

After my strange but helpful one-sided conversations with family and friends, I went to bed. I needed to sleep and get prepared for the following day. It felt like I had been in this crazy life forever, but we were nearing the end. There were only four more days to go. I wanted and needed to be at my best.

{ DAY 9 AND RAY EDWARDS }

When we, the remaining five, got to the set on Day Nine, we found out that this day's Hacker Safe Immunity Challenge would be our last.

I wasn't too surprised. I mean, how much longer could Joel go on giving daily immunity? At some point, he was going to be stuck having to eliminate someone he didn't want to eliminate simply because their teammate was wearing the shirt.

Our task was to go into a room alone (but surrounded by cameras, of course) and divvy up our remaining e-COMMerce chips based on who we thought would be the best person to do a JV with Joel. Oh, and we couldn't give any chips to ourselves.

I had no idea what the strategy was behind this one. Would he give immunity to the person with the most chips? The least?

The challenge was also more than a bit unfair as some of us had lots of chips while others had few. And since we couldn't vote for ourselves, we obviously had to put them somewhere. That meant that someone like me, who had the most chips left, would be populating the others' containers more than they could possibly be populating mine.

I decided to play it honestly — no strategy. That had been the way I played the rest of the competition, so why not? I considered every contestant and what they brought to the table — then thought about who I would JV with. Ultimately, I put four of my e-COMMerce chips in Charles' bucket and three in Thor's. I left

Alisande and Jason's containers alone as they both bring many of the same skills that I already have to the table. I know we were supposed to do it based on who Joel would JV with... but I didn't really know what he brings to the table other than a list (since I hadn't worked with him closely). I don't know, honestly, how anybody else split up their chips. Some people mentioned their splits, but I'll never know (unless it is aired) who really did what. All I know is that I didn't end up with very many chips in my container. Ouch — can't say that didn't hurt.

I think this phenomenon is probably the same with everybody, but I get a big flash of insecurity when I'm not picked first for something... whether it be for a team or if people think I should JV with Joel. I guess, because I'm competitive, I start to doubt my abilities and then immediately get angry. I doubted myself, and then that other people weren't recognizing my abilities. I suppose, if you're not already a confident person, not being picked first or being picked last, might just confirm your suspicions of inadequacy. And you would be brought down that way.

I don't understand people's need to be thought of as "great" by others. Our enormous need for acceptance is almost ridiculous. High school is a perfect example of that. I went to a very cliquey high school in Regina, O'Neill. But my problems weren't with high school...

Elementary school was an interesting study of human nature, female human nature to be more specific. I went to St. Mary, a French Immersion school. For those of you who don't know, Canada has two official languages (English and French) so we have many French Immersion schools throughout the country. It is not a pre-requisite that someone speak both languages. In fact, most French speakers live in the province of Quebec. In Canada, about 31 percent of the population can conduct a conversation in French. But that's an aside.

Because it was a French Immersion class, it was not large. In fact, there were only seven girls in my class (from kindergarten through to Grade Eight). The same seven girls: Kelly, Allison, Rachelle, Karen, Kerry, Nicky, and me. Our dynamic varied from year to year, but there was always one common factor. At least once, maybe twice every school year, there would be one girl who the rest of the group didn't talk to — AT ALL. It was strange.

The funny thing is that we all knew what it felt like to be *that* girl. Nobody wanted to be *that* girl. But, still, every year, we put a girl in *that* situation. It didn't really matter the reason — it changed all the time. Sometimes a girl became too bossy, sometimes she was too competitive, sometimes she was too skinny and didn't have boobs yet (me...). Whatever the reason, that girl was ignored by all of the other girls for months until they deemed her worth talking to again. Maybe it was because someone else in the group was now starting to bug them?

And it's not just female dynamics. The boy-girl thing is rough too. Same school, Grade Six. In Grade Five or Six, girls start to like boys, but boys aren't quite there yet. They're still in the GI Joe phase (or whatever boys do now before puberty — I don't know). Anyway, I liked some boy (why this boy — I have no clue). He, of course, didn't like me back. His loss, I'm sure — but whatever. All the girls knew I liked him and they had crushes of their own. So, at a school dance, somebody (I don't know who) requested a song for us. He ran out of the school gym, crying and embarrassed. Oh yes — he was a manly one. But you can imagine what it was like for me. Obviously, it sucked big time since Grade Six was almost twenty years ago.

Anyway, I digress... nobody likes being the odd man out. Having their flaws picked apart by other people. And, even though team leaders and group members might not be picking people apart aloud, mentally, they're still analyzing people's

171

strengths and weaknesses, and then selecting someone else. That's telling you that they don't think you're the best.

But, since there always has to be a "last," there's nothing that can be done about this. I just thought I'd bring it up since I think that other people probably feel the same way about it as I do.

So, back to the challenge… Thor had been given the most chips. He won… and we were all told by Eric that there would be no switching shirts that day. If you won the shirt — it was yours to keep.

Ray Edwards was our Classroom teacher that morning.

I was very excited because Ray is a copywriting expert and I am very interested in writing (duh). He specializes in online sales copy and direct sales websites, and this man is sought after. He has written for hundreds of different businesses in a wide variety of industries. In fact, his copy is known for making websites "obscenely profitable." That's a pretty good thing to be known for, in my opinion. He even writes for the gurus' (yes, some who have taught on NIM) websites. Ray frequently speaks at seminars on copywriting, promotions and marketing.

This was going to be good… His title was "Killer Copy Turns Words Into Wealth."

Ray said that the most important thing when writing copy is to connect to the emotions of the people you're writing to.

The process of buying is threefold:

1   Desire — you want to fill a need

2   Catches your eye — a specific product catches your attention

3   Persuade — you feed information into your mind about the product to persuade yourself to buy it

So then, what you as a writer need to figure out is the real leverage point in the psychology of your buyer. What is the real reason they are buying your product?

Once you figure that out, it's all about writing powerful, persuasive copy to convince the person to buy. Easy, right? No pressure, right?

But guess what? **Bad copy kills companies**.

This is the formula for online success:

Market + Product + Traffic + Copywriting = Profit

Copywriting is selling in print. It multiplies your sales and reduces your advertising costs.

You can use copywriting anywhere: email, e-Zines, auto responders, sales letters, squeeze pages, download pages, thank you letters, articles, blog posts, audio, and many more. Ray mainly focused on sales letters in his presentation to us.

A sales letter is a sales pitch in printed form.

You've probably seen sales letters before. I had. They're long. Unbelievably long. But I found out that's because you, as a writer, must answer each and every objection a person might have in advance. You have to anticipate all objections and possible questions from your buyer.

There is no one right way to write a sales letter (although when we were judged later on in the Execution Challenge, it appeared there definitely was a right and wrong way.)

There are fifteen basic elements of an online sales letter:

1 Pre-Head

2 Headline

3 Deck

4 Body

5 Subheads

6 Lead

7 Rapport

8 Credibility

9 Bullets

10 Testimonials

11 Value Justification

12 Risk Reversal

13 Bonus

14 Offer (call to action)

15 P.S.

The **pre-head** targets the prime prospects for your message. It's like the "eyebrow" of your headline. It might read something like… "Finally end your money worries forever… and I can prove it." It is in smaller print and above your headline.

Your **headline** is the ad for the rest of your ad. Its job is to get your reader to keep reading. It should be arresting and relatively short. You should be able to read it in two seconds. With the headline, you want to speak to the conversation that's already going on in your reader's mind. And you make it stand out.

The **deck** reinforces the impact of the idea proposed in the headline. It continues to arouse the reader's curiosity. It also builds credibility. The deck tends to be written in small print and is sometimes slightly darker than the rest of the text.

The **body** is the bulk of your text. The body will include many of the following elements.

Sub-heads are mini-headlines used to break up your text and keep your reader reading. No one likes to read long chunks of text so breaking it up using sub-heads is a good idea. Plus, many people only read headlines so the more you have, the more information your reader will get.

The first paragraph after the salutation is called the **lead**. The lead addresses whom the letter is for and what your reader stands to gain by reading it.

Build **rapport** with your reader. Rapport demonstrates that you know the reader's pain — that you understand their problems — that you can identify with them and share some common experiences.

Credibility answers "Why should I believe a single word you say?" That question is one of the top questions your reader will have about your proposal. Offer a sample of your clients and use quotes from them to prove your credibility.

The most important section of your sales letter is your **bullets**. Your reader will pay the most amount of attention to them. You want to write each bullet as a brief statement that identifies a single benefit offered by your product or service, but doesn't reveal how that benefit is derived. You want to tease, but not reveal. For example, "Three foods that will shave inches off your waistline… even Hollywood doesn't know them."

One of the biggest mistakes in writing a sales letter is not using enough bullets.

The secret of bullets is F.A.B.

F: features — something the product has

175

A: advantages — the advantage of the product

B: benefits — what the customer gets out of it

Testimonials answer the "Why should I believe you?" question. They are third-party verification that your solution does what it claims to do, from credible people who know. Testimonials are proof — and everybody loves proof.

Value justification highlights the value of your offer to the reader. It also contrasts it favorably with the price. Everybody wants to know that they're getting a deal and since you're not there to negotiate with, show them why the value of your offer is amazing.

Risk reversal removes the biggest obstacle in getting an order. Let your reader know that you're taking the risk… not them.

It also helps, and Ray is not sure why, to put a certificate-like border around the guarantee. It seems to add more authority and make it appear more genuine (not that it's not genuine.)

With risk reversals, watch the use of "100% Money-Back Guarantee". It's over-used. You should put it somewhere in your copy, but don't make it the focus. Find a different way of saying that you're taking the risk, not your reader. Something like "I Will Take All the Risk" or "You Risk Nothing… I Risk Everything." They say the same thing, but without the "lip service" of "100% Money-Back Guarantee."

Also, telling them that you are willing to give them their money back on your product shows that you have confidence in your product. Obviously, if everyone who bought your products asked for their money back, you couldn't stay in business. So your reader assumes that not too many people are asking for a refund (and hopefully they're right.).Don't be scared to offer that. Yes, you might have to give some money back, but you'll gain in client satisfaction. You don't need unhappy people bitching about you and your product.

A **bonus** is a related but unexpected gift that enhances the value of your offer. It shows that you're going the "extra mile" and helps push people from only "thinking" that they want to buy your product, to "needing" to buy your product.

Just watch that your bonus is related and that it is a value to your reader. Don't use the bonus section to unload junk.

Once people have read what you have to offer, you need an **offer**, a call to action. This is where you tell people what to do now that they're interested. It's where you ask for the order.

Using a dotted outline around this section works well.

You want to start this section with positive language in the reader's voice. Have a checkbox filled with a checkmark and text like "Yes, Jaime, I reserve my spot for Seminar A."

Then you want to spell out the benefits of your product again underneath.

Remember to also put your order link in the **P.S.** Sometimes people skip down directly to it and skip over most of your letter. Summarize the major benefits in your P.S.

Ray also gave us the **nine rules of copywriting that sells**:

1   Use all fifteen of the basic elements in your letter (no matter what the length)

2   Think always of your reader

3   Use short words

4   Use short sentences

5   Use short paragraphs

6   Establish credibility early (if you have credentials or expertise, mention that)

7 Repeat your core message with consistency

8 Use "aspirational" language. Everybody aspires to something. "If you've ever wanted to…"

9 Write like Socrates. You want to ask your potential readers a lot of questions before you start writing. Do some research about who might be buying the product and reading your letter. If you don't know what your readers might ask, it's going to be very difficult to answer their questions in your letter.

If you're in a rush to write your sales letter, this is a simple **four-part ad formula**:

1 **What** I'm selling

2 **Why** it's right for you

3 **Questions** you might have

4 What to do **now**

When you are copywriting, there are certain things you must do. The first is to go to where your prospects are. Find them… and listen to them. Engage them in conversation. Get their language. Find out their pain. After you get to know these people, then you can effectively write your sales letter.

After two hours and a lot of important information from Ray, we were ready for our Execution Challenge. That day, we would be three versus two. Team All-In only had two members left: Charles and me. It would certainly be wise for us to NOT end up in the Judgement Room.

Joel introduced Jen Groover, an entrepreneur who created a novel handbag called the Butler Bag.

Jen talked to us about her experiences with the creation, design and development of the bag. She also talked about how she had, so far, gone about marketing it.

She had the idea for the Butler Bag because it's virtually impossible for most women to find anything in their handbags. One night, while Jen was emptying her dishwasher, she put two and two together. Literally. What if there was something like a cutlery rack from the dishwasher inside your purse? That way everything would have a place and objects wouldn't slip out of the flimsy pockets most handbags come with. She took her dishwasher rack out of the machine, dumped out her handbag, and put the rack inside. It was exactly what she was looking for.

She worked for about a year and a half on the development of the bag before launching. And her idea caught on. Her bags had, thus far, been recognized in *Oprah Magazine*, by celebrities, and even in technology magazines. Jen was getting noticed.

But she was looking to greatly increase her sales on the web. She was looking for a sales letter. And guess who was going to write one?

If you guessed us, you're catching on to the game. Yes, teams All-In and Knuckle-Sandwich were each to write a sales letter about the Butler Bag.

Each team was loaned a bag and we were driven out to a mall. Our job was to gather testimonials about the bag — we needed these to include them in our letter: very important.

When we got back from the mall, which was absolutely dead (only 16 year olds and 60 year olds), we had four hours to write our letter.

I got to work writing as I had the most fashion knowledge and writing interest of our team. Charles put together a mock-up webpage where he put the sales letter and some pictures of the product. He also transcribed our testimonials. We worked well as a team… but it was very quiet. With only two people working — there's no talking. There's no need for it. I felt badly for the camera guys (not much to shoot).

I was pretty happy with our end result. I think Charles was too.

And I know that Knuckle-Sandwich were pretty nervous going up against us on this one. The first comment I heard from them after the assignment was handed out was "Can we have Jaime on our team?"

We presented our letter. Jen liked it. She thought it was written "girlfriend to girlfriend". Joel liked it for the most part, although he did think the call to action should have been more prominent.

Ray, on the other hand, tore it to shreds… I don't know whether he really hated it or was just playing it up for the cameras.

I was nervous. I had written the copy. My butt was on the line.

But I was confident that our letter was better than Knuckle-Sandwich's so I just sat there with my fingers crossed (not literally… well, maybe a second or two), and waited. Waited through the bashing from the judges.

And we won! Whew!

I was proud of my first attempt at writing a sales letter, so I was glad we won. But mostly I was relieved that I would not be going back into the Judgement Room. In fact, Charles and I were both quite pleased about that. The "one-trick pony" and the "new to everything" girl were not on the chopping block.

Instead we both received our own Butler Bag (which I use daily — thanks Jen!). Charles looked smashing with his. Actually, his girlfriend will find it quite handy, I'm sure, because… "Every girl needs a Butler."

We also both got copies of Ray Edwards' copywriting course. I WAS VERY EXCITED ABOUT THAT.

When Knuckle-Sandwich came out of the Judgement Room, only the two boys were left in the competition. Alisande had been eliminated. I don't know what went on in there (and I was glad not to have known), but I wasn't surprised, given the night before (when it had come down to Nico and Alisande's performances) at the judges' decision.

And now I was the only girl left in the competition. Me and three boys: Thor, Jason and Charles.

And, as far as I was concerned... it was anybody's game.

Throughout the competition, I was very grateful for Eric's family. His wife, Melissa, and her sisters, Kaitlyn and Hannah, were like family to me. They were and are so nice and genuine. I felt like they were my sisters. I don't know how I would have made it through without them. Seriously.

So I want to say a heartfelt "thank you" to all three of them.

It's so important to surround yourself with people who love and care for you. Although you might sometimes think you can do it alone, support is key to your success.

LIFE LESSON 11: Don't do it alone – build a support system.

My family is everything to me. Even though they all live two time zones away (except Ryan), I talk to at least one of them every day. They charge me up.

Sometimes we talk about stupid stuff. Sometimes we talk about relationships. Sometimes we get or give business advice. But whatever we talk about, I know it's a safe environment. They're never going to tell me that I'm an idiot or that I'm useless or that my ideas are dumb.

Now, don't get me wrong, they're not going to lie to me if they think my ideas are dumb. But they're going to find a more tactful and constructive way to tell me.

I have a few good friends who are exactly the same way. They support me 100 percent, even if they don't always agree with my choices.

The people who don't support you in life are better off left in your dust. I used to have a friend, quite a good friend actually. We did everything together when we were teenagers (good and bad stuff — we were each others' bad influences and safety nets.) We were so close.

And then our lives split paths. I moved away from the city. She didn't. But through that, we still remained friends. Pretty good friends, I think.

Then I started pursuing interests like acting and writing… and I don't think she understood. She definitely wasn't supportive of my ambitions or tactful. She's a 9-to-5 corporate girl, which there's nothing wrong with if that's what you want. But I think she thought that if you didn't have that kind of life, you were lazy, lived in dreamland, and would never amount to anything.

She never asked about how my acting was going.

Now, my relatives didn't all agree with my decision to go into acting either. Comments like "What are you going to do when you grow up?" and "So you're saying that you want to be a waitress forever, then?" were definitely made. But, the difference between my relatives and my "friend" is that they were supportive regardless of whether they agreed with my decision or not. They ask questions and listened to my experiences.

My friend never asked about my interests. And, if I brought them up, she quickly changed the subject. I never knew if it was because she was jealous or because she was rude or because she was selfish or because she just never knew how to talk about them, though she considered herself someone who could speak to any subject.

We have since pretty much lost contact. I still get the odd email from her, but I tend to respond very generally. I ultimately decided that her general negativity was just bringing me down. Often after we would speak on the phone, I would need to recharge afterwards. Who has time for that?

I never told her about the NIM competition, even after it had finished shooting. I highly doubt she would have thought it cool. I highly doubt that she would have been supportive. I might have been wrong, and if I am, then I'm so sorry, but my experience with her in the past taught me that she would have been dismissive and negative.

My guess is that if she knew that I had won the competition and was now a success — her reaction would be different than without the fame and fortune. But you don't want to be friends with people who are supportive because you're a proven success — you want to surround yourself with people who say "Hey — go for it! I'm behind you."

My amazing dad wrote me an email every day that I was in Colorado. They all went something like this:

Hello daughter dear

I know you can't tell me what you're doing or how you're feeling and I respect that. I just want you to know how proud your mother and I are of what you're doing. I know that you have the talent to win this thing. You're smart, creative and have a great person-

ality. And if Joel doesn't see that, then you don't want to work with him. But I know you'll do your best. You're such a hard worker and when you want something, you go out and grab it. I knew the very first time I heard about this competition that it was yours for the taking. I'm so proud of you.

And I want you to know that even if you have already been eliminated, just the fact that you made it to Colorado makes you a winner in our eyes. You had the courage to go and do something that not many people have the chance to do. You took the risk. Meet as many people as you can and make lots of friends.

Take advantage of every moment — and have a great time.

Love Dad and Mom

Every night, I came back to the hotel to read an email like that. How's that for support?

LIFE LESSON 12: Cut loose of negative vibes.

When I attended the Millionaire Mind Intensive (MMI) by Peaks Potentials, they really pushed mind philosophies, like the ones found in The Secret.

Picture your success (and be specific.) Write it down. Repeat this every day.

But you can't just wish for something and have it automatically happen. You have to be responsible for your own future.

At the MMI, we learned how to divide up our earnings in order to best move forward towards your ultimate goals. Every day, they told us, divide up your earnings and put them into jars. The following is the breakdown of how Peaks suggests you split up your money.

55% — Necessities

10% — Play

10% — Education

10% — Financial Freedom

10% — Long Term Savings

5% — Give Back

I started using this method before escaping my cubicle. I didn't use jars, they were not convenient for me. Like most 9-to-5ers, I got paid bi-weekly through direct deposit into my bank account so I used Excel spreadsheets and ING (www.ingdirect.com) accounts.

Very painstakingly, I actually figured out how much money I pulled in every day... after taxes. From there, I divided up my money from every paycheck and transferred that amount into my ING account. On an Excel spreadsheet, I split my ING up into the aforementioned accounts. That way, I could keep track of how much money was where. The system worked incredibly well for me.

You don't have to keep the percentages if they don't work for you. Change them up. If you NEED 60% for necessities, pull from some other accounts to make that happen. You should, however, scrutinize what you consider your necessities. Can you cut back anywhere? Making sacrifices sucks — I can tell you that from experience. I lived with roommates for five years to cut back on spending. But I did it, and now I'm ahead of the game. Remember — sacrifice now, but eventually you'll get to the point where you can have whatever you want.

The Necessities "jar" is for all *necessary* (for lack of a more creative word) things. These are things like mortgage/rent, car payment, transit pass, food, toiletries, basic necessities in clothing and shoes, coffee, bills, etc.

I didn't have enough in my Necessities account for everything that I thought was necessary, so some of my other jars became supplements to the Necessities jar.

The Play jar is meant for pure fun. It's meant to spoil yourself and do things you might never normally do. The thing about the Play jar is that you MUST spend it all every month. Just take it and do something crazy. Go for a spa day. Go to a restaurant and order whatever you'd like. Take somebody else out. Or buy an expensive pair of shoes.

That's what Peaks says to do with the Play jar. For me, because I'm a bit of a shop-a-holic, my Play jar supplements my monthly Necessities jar... And I NEVER have a problem spending it every month.

I think the Play jar is really meant for those people who are savers. Since I am not one of those people, it's hard for me to imagine having to be made to spend money. But if you're a saver, splurge. Use that Play account and don't feel the least bit guilty.

With regards to how people are with money, we fall into four categories:

1 Spenders

2 Savers

3 Avoiders

4 Monks

I am a spender. Spenders love to spend money. It makes them feel good. Spenders are therefore often in debt.

186

Savers, on the other hand, feel guilty spending money on themselves. They like to save in case of a rainy day.

My dad's a spender and my mom's a saver. You can imagine the fun they went through. The more my dad spent, the more my mom didn't. And the worse she felt. Eventually, they set up the jar system. Now, my dad is reined in (not fun, I'm sure, but responsible) and my mom has to spend. She goes for massages, on trips to Toronto, to Mexico with friends. Sometimes, because she loves him so much, she treats my dad (since his money was long spent) so he can enjoy too.

Avoiders like to stick their heads in the sand when it comes to money. They let bills pile up. They don't open bank statements. Really, they just want to ignore the whole issue.

Monks are above money. There are very few monks compared to the other three categories. It's a spiritual category and they just feel that it's beneath them.

LIFE LESSON 13: Spoil yourself at least once a month.

The Education jar is meant for courses, seminars, books, DVDs, whatever will help you further your knowledge and, therefore, your financial situation. If taking a university course is what you need, use your money that way. If you want to buy a membership to join a web-coaching club, use your Education jar for that. Anything… anything that helps you grow is what this jar is for.

Your Financial Freedom Account (FFA) is where you put your money and never spend it. It is the money you invest, the money that will eventually give you the passive income that will support you and let you stop doing any kind of work you dislike. You'll be able to do whatever you like.

187

Never forget to put money in your FFA jar. Even if you are in debt, Peaks says to put money in your FFA jar before paying off what you owe. Sure, it will take you longer to pay off your debt, but, when you do, you won't be starting from square one. You'll have a pot of money working for you.

It's depressing to look at the stats of how much money you can earn when you invest blank amount of money for blank amount of years if you haven't already been doing it. If you've ever seen one of those charts, you'll have noticed that the longer you have your money invested, the better. In fact, your total will by far surpass someone who has had their money invested for even five years less than you. Keep that in mind when you're thinking about using that FFA money to pay just a bit over your minimum debt payments simply to try and get it down faster.

Long-Term Savings (LTSS) is for objects that you want to or need to save for. I have my LTSS split into four categories. They don't build up quickly, but they're steady. Every day I put money into an LTSS-Home (for buying furniture and house stuff), LTSS-Vacation (yes, for going on vacations), LTSS-Me (this is more money for my Necessities — you can see I love to live beyond my means), and LTSS-Debt (this amount gets put onto my debt).

You can put it all onto your debt if you need to. You can do whatever. This is your money. Like I said, I split mine into four accounts. But, I can change that whenever I like. If I decide that I want to save for a down-payment for a house, then I might eliminate all three other categories and just work on the house.

Give Back is the final jar. It is for what it says. When you have money, it's good to give back to the people who are in need. Whether they are sick or poor, helping others builds your character and shows that you are about more than just making money — you are willing to give back to society.

I really admire people who give and I look forward to the day when I can do more of it. You can give in so many ways. Two sisters, both friends of mine, took their mother to a spa for her 50th birthday. One sister, Jen, was working two jobs, saving up for a house and a car, so she decided not to have any spa services that weekend. She spent her money taking time off to go, and putting in her half of their mother's trip. Her sister, Lisa, who lives alone and has a pretty good job, thought that Jen worked really hard and deserved a break. So, she bought two spa treatments for her sister. Lisa spent her money "giving" to someone else to make them feel good.

Sometimes when you're in the mode of saving, saving, saving, thinking of someone else and spending your money on them can seem ludicrous. That's why that Give Back jar is such a good idea. If, at the end of the month, or at the end of three months, there is $25, $250, or $25,000 in there — find a way that you can do something special for somebody else… and give knowing that all your other finances are in order.

Peaks also taught wonderful methodologies for getting rid of negative thoughts that enter our minds. I'm going to share a couple that I really liked. (I've made up the names, they don't come from Peaks.)

The Confidant. Negative thoughts are your own worst enemy. But often, they don't make a bit of sense. To destroy your negative thoughts and turn them around, debate them.

Have a friend recite one of your negative thoughts to you like it's their own idea. Look them right in the eyes while they're talking. After you hear them state your comment, tell them exactly why that doesn't make sense. It might sound weird, but hearing somebody else's problems and giving advice is something we, as people, do well. If you treat your own problems, thoughts, and ideas like that — you'll see how silly they really are.

189

For example, one of my negative thoughts is "I want to succeed, but if I try really hard and fail, then I'll know I'm no good." So, I stand with my sister, Stacey...

Stacey: "I want to succeed, but if I try really hard and fail, then I'll know I'm no good."

Jaime: "Maybe. But if you never try, then you'll never even have a chance at succeeding. Then where will you be?"

Stacey: "True. But, if I fail, then what will I do? Everyone will know that I'm not as smart as I thought I was."

Jaime: "But you are smart... and you can't succeed if you don't try. Why are you robbing yourself of the opportunity?"

And so on, and so on. You get the picture. Talk to your friend and you'll see how silly the problem really is. And you'll notice how, when it's not your problem, you see the big picture and have a lot of good advice to offer.

The Elastic Band. Put a thick elastic band around your wrist. Every time you say or think a negative thought, grab the elastic, pull it back a few inches, then let go. Beware...this will sting and leave a red mark. After you snap, you recognize the negativity and you replace it. Mark my words. You'll soon see a change in mindset. You're reshaping the way you think. Fear of pain... it works.

Peaks also goes back to what Mark Joyner talked about — setting goals and following steps. It is so cool how everybody's ideas and teachings work together — just like the body. Everything weaves intricately together to work.

{ DAVE TAYLOR }

O n the tenth day, it blew up. Tensions were high — and tempers were beginning to flare. There were explosions that morning before I even ate breakfast. (By the way, on a side note, my daily breakfast of egg-beater scrambled eggs was getting really disgusting.)

When I came down to breakfast, Thor and Charles were eating. Jason was not around, but there was a full plate of food and an empty chair with his name on it.

Apparently, he and Thor had been yelling at each other only moments before I came into the dining room, and then Jason had stormed away. Nobody knew where he had gone... and there were rumors that he had, perhaps, decided to leave the show.

I'm not sure exactly what their argument was about. It sounds gossipy to report on what I heard rather than what I saw, but I heard that the argument had something to do with the team of Alisande, Jason and Thor — and their previous night's loss. I believe there was some over-analyzing of the performance and some finger-pointing over contestants' motives both during the challenge and in the Judgement Room. Not good. Close quarters, hurt feelings and exhaustion are not a good combination. Mix that up with a quarter cup of homesickness and you've whipped up one big mess.

We found Jason outside reading scripture. Jason is very religious. I am not. I have my beliefs, but they are not something that, for me, are very prominent. I will say that, although we live differently, Jason is a very nice person. He does not push his beliefs onto other people. They are something that he chooses to live by — and he talks about them when he needs to, or when people ask. But he doesn't push.

I have a religious aunt. She pushes. She does nothing for herself — and then expects that God will lead her where she should go. And whatever happens to her is "God's will." I believe that God wants you to get off your butt and figure things out for yourself. There are 6.6 billion people in this world — God doesn't have time to give everybody exactly what they want and need. I think He respects some initiative. He gave us brains, after all.

That said, Jason is great. He is very funny. He reminds me a lot of Robin Williams. And he kept me in wide-eyed wonder at his magic tricks the entire competition.

Jason got into the car and we were off to the COMMplex. It was going to be an interesting day. Unless they changed the teams, it would be me and Charles versus Thor and Jason. With their pre-OJ squabble, who knew how they would work together? And that could only benefit Team All-In.

The day started out differently than the others. There was no Hacker Safe Immunity Challenge. As Joel had said, there would be no more. Nobody would be immune. That was a good thing. It would really suck if your partner was immune and your team lost. I mean, why go into the Judgement Room? They really might as well just say "Oh, I guess you're gone."

Dave Taylor was our Classroom speaker that morning.

Dave is a really smart guy. He holds a Bachelor's degree in Computer Science, a Master's in Educational Computing and an MBA. And he has received a variety of academic and professional honors throughout his twenty-five year career. Dave has been involved in blogging and the world of blogs since 2003. His AskDaveTaylor.com tech support site gets almost one million unique visitors each month. He is a well-known speaker and frequently speaks about blogs and social networks to audiences of all sizes.

Dave was going to be talking to us about Blogging and Web 2.0.

I've already talked about blogging in this book. Let me say a few words about Web 2.0.

First off, I have a funny story about Web 2.0. In my JOB, earlier this year, we started a webinar called "Bring Your Intranet Into The 21st Century". Makes sense, right? You want to be up to date with technology.

Our Intranet currently is in a content management system (CMS). That means that it's a template system that allows non-techy people to easily publish content on the site. For the publishers, it works like Word. The web team manages the back end of the CMS and does some HTML coding behind the scenes.

The Intranet itself isn't too fancy. It's relatively attractive, but, technology-wise, it is, as all government Intranets are, very behind the times. They have a couple of podcasts, a couple of videos, some surveys, and lots of pictures and text.

And that's fine. Whatever. It serves its purpose for the employees. I doubt the government employees are ready for more anyway. Certainly, with the multitude of approval layers needed to publish content, nothing spontaneous like a forum or blog would really work anyway.

But back to the webinar. It talked about Web 2.0. Blogging, social networks, wikis, forums, video. Had anybody in the webinar (six people) been on a blog? No. Had anybody been on You Tube? One — once. Did anybody have a Facebook or MySpace account? No.

Obviously I said yes to all — except blogging.

But the "expert" web team didn't know. Had no clue. And they get paid like $75,000 per year! Wow. (Sorry, had to blow off some steam about that. It shocked me, really, but not really.) How can you do your job if you don't know the world you work in… shocking! That's a union environment for you.

Web 2.0 is defined by Wikipedia as:

"Alluding to the version-numbers that commonly designate software upgrades, the phrase "Web 2.0" may hint at an improved form of the World Wide Web. Advocates of the concept suggest that technologies such as weblogs, social bookmarking, wikis, podcasts, RSS feeds (and other forms of many-to-many publishing), social software, Web APIs, Web standards and online Web services imply a significant change in web usage."

1.0 vs. 2.0

Web 1.0	Web 2.0
Double Click	Google AdSense
Ofoto	Flickr
Akamai	BitTorrent
Mp3.com	Napster
Britannica Online	Wikipedia
Personal website	Blogging
Evite	Upcoming.org and EVDB
Domain name speculation	Search engine optimization
Page views	Cost per click
Screen scraping	Web services
Publishing	Participation
Content management systems	Wikis
Directories (taxonomy)	Tagging (folksonomy)
Stickiness	Syndication

"If you can't be found… you're already dead."

~Dave Taylor

That quote is so true. You can have the best site in the world. On it, you can offer the best products. At the best price. And if nobody can find you, if they don't know you exist, you're screwed.

Using Web 2.0 — you can really work to get your name and your site out there.

A **blog** is really just a tool.

Blog attributes:

» Cheaper than a website

» More search engine friendly

» Easy to manage

» Fun to produce

» Used to establish a dialogue with your customers (think focus group)

» Others produce your content

You can even you use blogging to survey your customers. You just ask a question in the blog and people will post comments on it.

There are pitfalls to blogging, such as:

» Dealing with whiney bloggers

» Expectations of frequent updates

» Saying too much

» Spammers

» Being suckered into using digital polluters (machine-generated junk)

» Creating un-indexable content

The following are some smart blogging techniques:

» Allow comments

» Have an authentic voice

» Identify your bias and relationships

» Establish credibility

» Write about what you know

» Share testimonials

» Follow your industry and market news

» Stay focused (keep your blogs to one subject)

So what can you write about in a blog? Answer: ANYTHING. Pick a subject that you're interested in and write. Chances are, if you are interested — other people will be too.

Best practices in blogging:

» Write about your product infrequently (talk about other interesting stuff)

» Write at least two articles per week

» Each article should be at least two hundred and fifty words

» If you can, add pictures

» Avoid grammatical and spelling errors (they stand out glaringly and make you look amateurish)

Once you have a blog — you're not done. Obviously, people have to find out about it. One way is to add the URL to your signature. Then you can visit forums and post comments. Or you can visit other people's blogs and leave comments. Just make sure your comments add value to the site. Otherwise, why would anyone want to see what you have to say on your own site? Be knowledgeable and witty.

There are a lot of very popular blogs out there. You can find them using websites like Technorati.com (it gives you an authority ranking on blogs), or you can use blogsearch.google.com.

Just make sure that when you comment on other people blogs, your comments are relevant. Don't go and plug your site or product. In fact, you might not even want to mention your site until you've established a relationship.

Sometimes when unwelcome and unwarranted comments are made to a blog, the owner will ban the commenter from ever again posting a comment. That's why it's imperative that the comments be valid and useful. It would be such a waste to get banned.

So, how do you comment then? Well, it's important to write good, thoughtful, relevant, valuable and interesting additions to the discussion. If your post looks spammy — it will get removed.

Social Networks are huge in Web 2.0.

Currently the **top four social networking sites** are:

1   MySpace

2   Facebook

3   Second Life

4   LinkedIn (professional networking site)

Definitely get a presence on these sites.

I have a Facebook account. At first, I fought it. I'd get friend requests to join and I'd think "What the hell?", and delete them. I thought it was some kind of spam program trying to get my information. And a big waste of time.

Then my friend, Jen (a different friend Jen), signed me up at work one day (that was before the provincial government blocked MySpace, Facebook, and You Tube from their computers). I still thought it was a joke. But then I started connecting with people and my obsession with Facebook grew.

It was amazing. I was having conversations with my 14 year-old cousin, Nicole, who I rarely see or talk to. I chatted with my aunt in London, England (to phone her regularly would just break me). And the best part was that I could see what my friends were up to without initiating dialogue. It's quick and easy. That's how, for me, social networks started beating out email.

That's the "old-person" argument with Instant Messaging and social networks: "Why don't you just email?" And they're right — to a certain extent.

But it goes way deeper than email. Like I was saying, my friends can post their "status" (how they're feeling or what they're doing). Even though they're not doing anything pointing towards me, I can immediately see that "Stacey is feeling really full of puffed wheat cake." "Philip is officially counting days left at work. There are five," and "Tara is fighting a cold...and might be losing...." when I open my account.

I can also see picture albums that my friends put up or search for old friends from school or work. It's amazing. I just touched base with a girl from my old dancing days and found out what almost every member of my old team is up to now. In my head, they're all 10 to 15 years old because that's what they were the last time I saw them. Now, some have children, some are married, some are traveling, one lives in New Zealand. It's crazy! Sometimes I feel like I've done so much — but I expect the people I grew up with to be doing what they were doing when I last saw them. But everybody moves on and hearing about all of their life experiences is just "wow."

So, yes, Web 2.0 — good thing.

The essence of Web 2.0 can be found in these sites:

1   You Tube

2   Digg

3   Delicious

4   Squidoo

5   Flickr (pictures)

6   Blogs

With the two-hour Classroom session over and done, Joel announced the Execution Challenge of the day. And it was a doozie.

IT WAS AN EIGHT HOUR CHALLENGE.

Eight hours is long. It's longer than a typical government work day… Let's just say it's a really long time to sit and not move.

Our mission was to get unique visitors and links to a web page for Hearts and Hands International.

Hearts and Hands International is a non-profit charity foundation that helps children at risk around the world. Hearts and Hands assists by providing programs and volunteer teams to help with needs of children. They are a really valuable organization. If you want to help them out, their website is www.heartsandhandsinternational.org.

The judging would work as such… we would get 10 points per unique visit to the site, and 100 points per web link to the site by bloggers. Each team had a special Hearts and Hands page set up to count everything.

Obviously, we had to use Web 2.0 methods to get our message across. We could also monitor the other team's number of unique visitors (although we only checked from one computer so as to not give them another 10 points.)

We also couldn't hit up anybody we knew by being ourselves. That sucked because if we could have used Trippy's lists, we would have soared big time.

So Charles and I got down to work. Luckily, we hit some social networking sites that worked for us and we started getting visits. We knew that Knuckle-Sandwich was way behind us in number of visits, but we had no idea about their number of links to. Ultimately, we only ended up getting one.

The challenge was long, but not long (if that makes any sense.) It wasn't stressful, but we were done with it long before it was over.

I don't know if the NIM producers were looking to test our endurance or whether or not we had Attention Deficit Disorder (ADD). But spending eight hours staring at the computer screen without blinking, in absolute silence, is not fun. I think we were all pretty disoriented when we were done.

In the end, Knuckle-Sandwich and All-In tied. Knuckle-Sandwich used chat rooms on MySpace to get lots of link backs to their site. They were pretending to chat up men as a 30 year-old blonde chick in order to get them to do what they wanted. That didn't particularly impress the judges. Also, it was found that some of their links weren't really functional, so they had 300 points deducted... and All-In won.

No prize today — just immunity. That sucked... but it felt good that we helped out the charity. Hopefully, we actually brought in some awareness for the cause.

When Jason and Thor went into the Judgement Room that night, I had no idea who would emerge as the one staying and who would be going home. They both have strengths and weaknesses. And Joel had already narrowed down our playing field so much. All who were left were relatively strong.

Charles and I just sat and waited.

And waited.

And waited.

Then Jason stormed into the waiting area, tears in his eyes. He was mad.

Thor followed behind him and kind of gave us the knowing look that said "Jason was eliminated." Both Charles and I went up to Jason to offer sympathy. He wasn't quite ready for it. He left the COMMplex to sort things out.

It was then that we heard what really happened in the Judgement Room. In fact, the judges hadn't eliminated Jason, he had eliminated himself.

Joel was going through his spiel, his regular Judgement Room speech, about who should go and who should stay. Apparently, Jason just said to him "You know what — I don't want to do a joint venture with you." He just cracked.

The pressure in that room is pretty incredible if you let it be. And night after night of being in pressure-filled situations can kill someone. Obviously, Jason didn't really feel that he didn't want to work with Joel Comm — he wouldn't have been in the competition if he had. But he snapped. And ruined it for himself.

I was talking with one of the judges afterwards. He told me that the panel had been leaning towards eliminating Thor and that Jason's outburst came out of nowhere — bam! It really threw everything off.

LIFE LESSON 14: Never quit — even if the going gets tough.

You never know what people are thinking. Even if you think you might know — you don't. So don't make their decisions for them. And never, never lose your cool.

Again, you don't know what other people are thinking. Don't let your insecurities fester to make you do something you'll later regret. It's not worth it. You'll often be the person who thinks the worst of yourself. You'll often be the person who most notices your mistakes. So guess what?

DON'T POINT THEM OUT TO OTHER PEOPLE.

Hello — let them figure things out for themselves.

You know those people who say "My thighs are so fat." So, of course, you look at them. And you say "Oh no, they're not." But you think "Hmm — I hadn't noticed before, but now that you've pointed it out, you're right, your thighs are fat."

You also don't know the other side of the story. When Jason lost his temper, he had no idea what the judges were really thinking about Thor. Would he have held it in if he had known? I guess we'll never know. But I would have.

It's funny. People think that they are first and foremost in other people's minds. I have a friend who has to buy a new dress for every party she attends. Why? Because "I've already worn this dress — and people will remember." Really? It's been a long time between wears. Quite honestly, I can't remember what most of my co-workers wore yesterday. But she thinks that she's important enough that people will remember everything that she does at all times... because she remembers what she does.

I asked her if she remembered what other people wore to the party the previous year. "No, but that's different...," was her reply. Different how? I never did get an answer. Maybe because

DAY 10 AND DAVE TAYLOR

203

she thinks that she looks better in a dress than her colleagues, people will remember. But I doubt they will... I think that's a little "You're so vain; you probably think this song is about you."

So, anyway, regardless of the reason for Jason's freakout, we were down to three. Charles, Thor, and me. I was so proud of myself. I even gave myself a pat on the back to recognize my success — hey, that's what they tell you to do in Peaks. I know, it sounds silly. But I'm really starting to buy into that silly-sounding stuff. It's working.

Out of the three, I had no clue who would win. But I guess there were only two more days left to figure that out. Oh well, I wouldn't have to be curious for long.

At this point, I was really hoping that they would tell us the ultimate winner. I had heard, at one point, that the winner was going to be announced at a live ceremony in Las Vegas (or some-where) in November. That would really have sucked.

{ DAY 11 AND PERRY MARSHALL }

Friday morning, we were rushed immediately into the Classroom with Perry Marshall.

Perry is known as "The Wizard of Google AdWords." He is one of the world's leading specialists on buying search engine traffic. In fact, he's so good, that Google advertisers who use his methods generate over half a billion clicks per month... and that's a conservative estimate! Perry runs a consulting firm, Perry S. Marshall & Associates, and has published dozens of articles on sales, marketing and technology. *Guerrilla Marketing for Hi-Tech Sales People* and *The Definitive Guide to Google AdWords* are a couple of his works. He also speaks at conferences around the world.

Perry talked about the 80/20 rule. This rule is the law of nature and the way it works in business is this: 80 percent of your business comes from 20 percent of your customers. But guess what? Everything can be broken down into this 80/20 rule. It's really cool.

If 80 percent of your business comes from 20 percent of your customers, then 20 percent of your business comes from 80 percent of your customers, right?

Take that a step further... Out of that top 20 percent, if 20 percent of that group does 80 percent of that group's spending, that would be the top four percent of your total customers making up about 64 percent of your sales.

So:

» 20% spend 80%

» 4% spend 64%

» 0.8% spend 52%

That means that less than one percent of your customers represents over half of your sales!

Why would you spend all your advertising dollars on these guys? The biggest problem that most businesses make is that they spend too much money trying to get new customers... when the majority of their sales come from regulars. They should be spending 80 percent of their advertising money on the 20 percent who are these regulars. Then you end up with really happy, dedicated customers who advertise for you by word-of-mouth.

In guerrilla marketing, the:

» Principle is always true

» Technique is something you do in a particular situation that might work.

The best advertising appeals to **primal emotions**:

» Pride

» Fear

» Competition (to be the best)

» Sensual gratification (sex, food, beauty)

Just think about *Cosmopolitan* Magazine. It sells incredibly well. For one thing, the super-market check-out lane is the best real-estate for magazines, candy, etc. It's impulse buying at its best. And *Cosmo* is the most popular check-out magazine. But, why is that?

Well, *Cosmo* covers are brilliant. So brilliant that they have been studied — there is a huge psychology behind them. More work is put into the *Cosmo* cover than anywhere else in the magazine. There's always the hot chick, the boobs, the strategically placed headlines that target insecurities. The covers grab your attention and tell you where to look, where to look next, and next, and next... until you just have to buy.

Obviously, we don't all want magazines like *Cosmo* for our business, but you can take the concept and switch it up to fit your company. Grab your customer's attention, make them look, keep them looking...

But, seriously, take a look at a Cosmo cover... you'll see what I'm talking about.

Primal emotions can be used in any form of advertising, even small ads with a limited number of words. For instance, in Google Ads you're looking at 120 characters or less. The following is a really good Google Ad:

Coffee Exposed

A secret that coffee co's

don't want you to know

www.coffeefool.com

Interestingly enough, Google Ads are about the same amount of text as a *Cosmo* headline. Things that make you go hmmmmm...

Try to make use of publicity to promote your business. Write a press release. Most people are intimidated by reporters. But really, all you have to do is make what you do interesting and wrap a story around it... publicity will find you.

Just ask yourself "What is the story behind the story?" What's the Jerry Springer? What's interesting?

Most reporters won't dig for a story. They just don't have the time. If you issue a press release with an interesting hook — you're basically handing them an article. Most reporters will jump at that. All they should have to do is give you a quick call — and voila — story.

A friend of mine used to work for a popular Canadian news-radio station. They had daily "story meetings" where they had to pitch ideas to the bosses. It's pretty hard to come up with idea after idea. My friend found this story meeting the most intimidating and stressful part of her job. She hated going into the meeting without an idea. And she always wanted to have two or three in her pocket just in case the first one was shot down. I'm sure she would agree with me — well-written press releases made her job a whole lot easier.

LIFE LESSON 16: Find an interesting hook to everything you do in life.

Trust me, the hook is there. And if you find it… it's gold. If I was better at finding that hook, I'd be way further ahead in life.

Think about it this way… hundreds of thousands of girls want to be actresses. Probably 80 percent of them are thin, blonde and 20 something. Hmmm — who to choose? Well, if you have an interesting hook — then you can stand out from the crowd. I didn't find that hook, but if I had even known to look for it… who knows where I would be now? I might not have become the next Gwyneth Paltrow… but I might have been part of the forensic unit of CSI, or even a regular day-player jumping around from

208

show to show. Whatever, the point is that I didn't try to play off anything. I just expected my talent to get me noticed. And it did... but it only took me so far. The hook! So important.

Widgets or widgetizing is taking something that's familiar and twisting it around so, suddenly, it's not the same as everything else out there.

For example, think about the iPod. There were other mp3 players out there before the iPod. But then, Apple pushed the new iPod... they made iTunes, changed the shape of the mp3 players, charged for songs. They made everything easy — and they took over the market.

Never cut the price — add value instead.

Don't sell a-la-carte — sell in packages. Combine product and services in one.

When you've bundled products — create an experience for your customer.

Think about Starbucks... Okay, coffee is cheap. I know this. I even have a coffee maker in my cupboard. I have travel cups. I could make my coffee for probably under five cents every day. But, instead, I choose to spend $4.73 every day on my coffee. Why? Because Starbucks created the whole coffee experience.

They turned coffee gourmet. They decorated the store with comfy chairs. They played music. They took "small", "medium" and "large", and called them "tall", "grande" and "venti". They turned coffee into a luxury. One that almost everybody can afford. And, it's a bit of a status thing. I know I feel good about my coffee choice when I walk around with my little white cup with green print. I even share a knowing look of superiority with other people carrying their Starbucks cups.

Starbucks created an experience. An experience that people, like me, obviously pay $4.68 for every day (I've subtracted the five cents it would have cost me to make my daily latte).

So what are they pushing, as far as primal emotions go? Pride, competition and sensual gratification. Not bad.

In Toronto, there is a lot of competition for coffee places. We have Starbucks, Second Cup (the Canadian Starbucks), Tim Hortons, Timothy's, and the assortment of mom & pop places you find anywhere. They litter every street corner. We Torontonians really like our coffee.

It's funny, I went to Winnipeg, Manitoba to visit relatives and felt a bit like Paris Hilton (God forbid!). Yes, I was such a "city-girl" trying to search out a Starbucks for my daily fix. But nothing…I was starting to panic. Finally I sat back and listened to myself and thought, *oh, shut up*. And I did. Only then did a Starbucks emerge. But, the point of this story is that in Winnipeg, it's not coffee places on every street corner. THERE ARE FAST FOOD JOINTS EVERWHERE. It was disgusting. There you go — that's my two cents. I apologize, but, since I'm writing this book, sometimes you have to read about my pet peeves. **Fast food is not food.**

Now that my little rant is over, Microsoft is another example of an experience product. Okay, you buy a computer that uses Microsoft Windows. Then you need to buy Microsoft Office (Word, Excel, Power Point, Outlook). You can create documents, but for others to be able to view them, they need to have Microsoft Office. You get?

Kid Snips is a haircutting place in Chicago. Sure, parents can take their kids to any haircutting place. It's pretty cheap. At Kid Snips, though, the kids get to sit in a car while they get their hair cut. They get to watch a video instead of staring at themselves in a mirror. They get a free little toy at the end. And it costs way more than most other places charge for kids' haircuts. AND PARENTS PAY IT — for the experience. Kid Snips totally widgetized haircuts.

If you send emails to your customers — you are in the entertainment industry. It is your job to entertain your clients just like it's Oprah's job to entertain her viewers.

Your emails need to be relatable. Have you ever wondered why people like Oprah? It's because she's human. She has had public problems and she admits them. She's not like these starlets who are in and out of rehab — denying that anything is wrong with them. Oprah says "I have a problem with food," and people like her.

You want to start your emails with a story or something personal. It will create an emotional bond. Your goal is to create emails that people look forward to getting. Emails that excite people when they arrive in their box.

Every year, I write a Christmas letter and send it out to my family and friends. I don't have time to write all of my news personally to everybody and I'm not the best at keeping in contact throughout the year. So, since I love the tradition of sending out physical cards (as opposed to email or eCards), I include a letter. I always try to make my letters very creative so that I grab the attention of people quickly. And every year I try to make them different. The best compliment I ever received on my letters was the one year I didn't have the time to write one (and I hadn't really felt like I'd done anything special to write about). My Aunt Alice asked my mom where my letter was because she had been so excited to get the envelope in the mail knowing that inside would be a great letter. Knowing that people looked forward to my letters made me feel amazing and much more enthusiastic to write

211

the following year. Just make your writing fun — and you will touch people.

Jaime's 2004 Christmas Letter

INT. ONTARIO PROVINCIAL GOVERNMENT OFFICE — MORNING

JAIME LUCHUCK, thin, blonde, 28 (gasp), is sitting at her desk. There is no work to be found in her department so she sits, trying not to look bored and desperately trying to busy herself.

BEN, 24, enters the office. He is Jaime's counterpart in her department. Ben is a typical government worker. He doesn't at all mind having nothing to do. In fact, he thrives on it. Jaime has nicknamed him the Pillsbury Dough Boy. She thinks that if pressed in the stomach, Ben would "hee hee."

BEN

Morning Jamie…

(in the office, everyone spells Jaime's name wrong)

Oh, no work… okay.

Ben leaves his desk; heading towards the kitchen to make his breakfast.

Jaime leans back in her chair, deep in thought. Since this act might get her into trouble, she decides to write a Christmas letter. It is December 2. She opens up her script writing software (because she bought it and, damn it, it was expensive so she's going to use it) and begins typing.

JAIME

Hello everyone. I hate sending out a mass
Christmas letter but, well, you all know how it is.

Ben returns.

BEN

Jamie, can I borrow your can opener?

*Jaime opens her desk drawer and gives him her can
opener. Ben lopes out of scene with a dopey smile on
his face. Jaime goes back to her keyboard.*

JAIME

This year has been a "forward" year which is
always good. I'll start at the beginning.

In February, blah blah blah…

*DAVID, 35, comes by Jaime's desk to drop off
some work.*

INT. ONTARIO PROVINCIAL GOVERNMENT
OFFICE — MOMENTS LATER

*With the work that David had dropped off done, Jaime
returns to her letter.*

JAIME

This fall, I opened my own production company.
Tired of playing the waiting game, blah blah blah…

Merry Christmas and Happy New Year to everyone.
Hopefully, if I don't see you, I will, at least, speak
with you during the holiday season.

Jaime leans back in her chair. She looks at the clock on her computer. It reads 9:44 a.m. She sighs with despair. Her regular thoughts about quitting pop into her head but she pushes them aside. If she wants another year like this past one, she better stay put and keep collecting that paycheck.

THE END

In your emails to customers, you also want to lead with information. That's one of the best ways to sell a product. If you have published a book, there is no better business card.

Position yourself as an expert. Having a book makes you stand out. See if experts will contribute to your book. See if they will then promote your book. Joel Comm wrote the foreword for this book — and he is an authority. I'm sure when you first looked at this book, you thought "Hey, if Joel thinks she's good — then she must be good". Of course, you would be right. But, seriously, "As seen on *blah, blah, blah (or Bob Loblaw for Arrested Development fans)* TV show" or whatever, is great to throw in right away.

For those of you who don't know much about marketing — don't worry. It's more important to know a market than about marketing. Let me repeat that because it's important:

It's more important to know a market than about marketing.

This is huge for me. I don't consider myself a marketer. Not yet, anyway. But there are some markets I do know. And I know how and what to sell to them. Health… that's one market I'm definitely going to tap. If you go to www.JaimeLuchuck.com (remember that's Jaime not Jamie), you can see what I've decided to do. All of my future sites will be linked through this website so it will really be my resume from now on. Keep checking and checking… it will only grow.

But I am definitely interested in markets as opposed to products. I doubt that I'll become an affiliate marketer. I like the hands-on aspect of helping people (my markets) with products I know will help them or that I know they'll enjoy.

So don't be intimidated because you're not a marketer. My brother (the music business brother) is not a marketer and he's doing really well so far. There are ways to educate yourself on marketing techniques. In fact, sometimes you get someone who considers themselves a marketer, but they really don't know their markets. And, if they're walking around trying to apply marketing techniques to the wrong markets, they'll be up you-know-which creek without a paddle.

After Perry spoke, we ate lunch (I had two huge plates of taco salad... after the previous day's eight-hour challenge, I was stocking up on fuel), it was time to hear about the Execution Challenge.

It was going to be another outdoor day. We were going to be giving away tickets to Over The Hedge, a Dreamworks animated movie about a con-artist raccoon who steals some food and has to repay it with his team of mismatched buddies. Bruce Willis is one of the voice actors. And Dreamworks films are usually pretty good. Hey — they did Shrek and Madagascar! "I like to move it, move it."

Anyway, we could give the tickets (yes, they were FREE) away anywhere in Loveland or Fort Collins that we wanted. It would be playing at dusk at the Loveland Fair. We were going to be judged on the number of people who actually showed up for the screening — not the number of tickets we gave away. Therefore, we were supposed to be smart about who we gave the tickets to. Each one was numbered so it would just be a matter of counting the tickets at the end.

215

There was another benefit to the tickets. There would be three cash draws before the film started. Twenty-five, $50, and $100 prizes would be another reason for people to actually show up.

Then the judges started talking about affiliates and how, in Internet marketing, your affiliates generate a great deal of your sales. We would, they told us, be getting some affiliates to work for us.

Great. I thought that since this was a kids' movie, we'd each get some kids to work with… but I was wrong. As we, the final three, were all wondering what the heck was going on, out walked the other nine contestants (back from the guest ranch.) They were going to be our affiliates.

It was so great to see them. I hadn't realized how much I had missed some of them until they were back. I hadn't really been given much time to miss them. But some of them, like Carly, Laura, and Steve, had become friends and they had been gone for over a week. Also, it was nice to be surrounded by people who had left the competition setting. I wasn't particularly close with the remaining people. Not because they're not nice people, but because circumstances hadn't brought us together. I hadn't worked with Thor, and, because neither of them are girls, we hadn't roomed together. You can really bond with people when you room together.

We got to build our affiliate teams by taking turns picking from the eliminated contestants. Nice — another round of team-picking. I didn't pick first, but I got most of the people I wanted. Actually, that sounds bad. Let's put it this way… I was happy with everybody I chose, I just would have also liked to have some of the others as well.

My first pick was Nico. He did an amazing job selling popsicles and since this was another "selling to kids" thing, I thought he'd be perfect. I was really happy he didn't get nabbed by the first picker (Thor). I picked Steve next, then Debbie. Nico asked me afterwards why I picked him — he said he was surprised by my decision. I don't know why he asked that. I hoped I hadn't given off the vibe that I didn't like him or thought that he was incompetent at our last encounter (in the Judgement Room when I picked him to go.) It's so nasty and relationship-destroying, that damn Judgement Room.

Another reason that it was nice to see the eliminated contestants was that I could give Alisande the flowers that were delivered to our room the day after she was gone. I have to admit I was a tad suspicious. She gets eliminated, talks to her husband, then she gets flowers. Hmmm… but I didn't say anything. I don't know if she told, if he guessed, if she just sounded rotten or if it was just pure coincidence. Whatever. I honestly believe most of the contestants will tell their spouses after they get home. It must be hard, when you're married or live with someone, not to tell them what happened. For me, it's just really fun watching people's reactions to the show. Remember, as I've been writing this book, the NIM finale hasn't been broadcast yet. Hearing their guesses and predictions makes not telling so worthwhile. Don't get me wrong, I'm not saying that any contestant told, as we were bound by a legal agreement not to. I'm just saying it would be extremely tough for them not to. Good for them if they didn't.

Nico had a great idea on how to use guerrilla marketing to "sell" our tickets. I mean, they were free, people didn't have to pay for them, but we needed them to show up so we really did have to sell the benefits. Anyway, Nico offered up a three-night stay at his resort in Costa Rica as a draw prize. I wasn't sure what the judges would think… but they went for it.

Out we went. We had 5 ? hours to give these things away. The market at the fair became saturated immediately. We left the grounds and tried to give and give and give.

217

Walmart was an interesting stop. We almost had the cops called since we were *soliciting* on their property. A "very dedicated employee" was making sure we left off the property and were staying off.

We went to the mall, to McDonalds, to Target, to a kids' haircutting place, a kids' store (another team beat us there though). Eventually, we went back to the fair.

Nico had a great idea and started stopping cars as they were coming into the fair. I'm going to repeat this... Nico did an amazing job getting rid of our tickets. And it meant a lot to me because he was helping ME out by doing this. He was already out of the competition — **he was helping me.**

I hate cold-calling, I already ranted on that subject earlier. Heather told me to act... she said that selling is just like acting. But I wasn't finding it. I don't like being a bother to people and I really just couldn't find a groove. I felt like a nuisance and I doubt you're supposed to feel that way when you're trying to sell. I just know my strengths and weaknesses and my strength is to either sell by writing or video... not cold-call. And my market is not mothers. Like I said, I can sell to men, and little kids usually like me... but I can't really relate to mothers. Plus, I feel stupid approaching them when I'm wearing business clothes and have cameras following me.

At least I had my face painted (by Kaitlyn's friend, thank you), which is something I had never had done before. It was purple and sparkly... I'm such a girl.

When we got back to the COMMplex, we were all pretty exhausted. It had been bright and sunny and brutally hot, and we'd been walking around all day. Dinner was served and we all chowed down. And waited to hear the results.

And then... it rained.

The movie was being shown outside and it rained. We couldn't believe it. So many people who would have gone… So many people who just left the fairgrounds or stayed home because of the weather… It really sucked.

> ## LIFE LESSON 17: Some things you just can't control. Deal and move on.

And we waited. And waited.

And waited.

Playing ping pong and foosball. Charles Trippy kicking some ping pong butt. Way to go!

Joel was getting pretty cranky. I think the long days were getting to everybody. A lot of the contestants were pretty concerned about him and what he was like in real life. To us, he was only who he was portraying on the show. Since I'd been on TV before, I was pretty sure that he was just acting out a character. But because we only saw him on set, we'd only seen this character. And it was getting old, I have to admit — sorry Joel, I'm just telling it like it was. By the way, Joel is really a great guy off the show. He is not his NIM character, for those of you who watched. At the wrap party, he dropped the character and we all had a great time together.

Finally the verdict was in.

"Quiet on the set"

"Roll tape… Action!"

We did our walk-in and got set up. Thor's team went onstage. Joel tore Thor apart, and his affiliates too, especially Christine. We were all a little shocked. Then it was my team's turn. We went up. The judges were okay. They picked on Debbie a bit, but then let us leave.

But then suddenly, we had to stop. Charles had got a pretty bad case of sunstroke and was in the bathroom throwing up. He had tried to come on set but he always ended up running back to the bathroom. I'm sure the hot lights weren't good for him either. I felt really badly for him — it totally sucks being sick. He did look a bit comical later on since they didn't have any ice on hand. He had to hold freezies to his head to cool himself off. Ahhh, if only someone had taken a video. It would be a sure You Tube hit.

After a long wait (but still no Charles), the judges decided that we would redo the entire judging segment the next morning and sent us all back to the hotel. I have to admit it kind of sucked not knowing the outcome. I'd have to get up early and get dressed, only to perhaps get eliminated. If I was going home, I would have liked at least one day to get some sleep. Early Sunday morning, I was going home and Monday was back to work. On the bright side — I had made it to the last episode regardless… and that was pretty cool.

And Joel apologized for being a bit cranky.

I had a great night that night with the old roommates. Having Carly and Laura back was so much fun. As it turns out, the Loser Lounge (as the eliminated contestants had dubbed it) was a great home up in the mountains. The eliminated contestants went for massages, went alpine sliding, shopped, went out to eat, spent time in the hot tub, talked with a guru about their futures and networked a lot with each other. It sounded like a great time, and I kind of feel like I missed out. I wanted to make sure I kept in touch with them after NIM to learn what they know. Not that I was unhappy to be in the top three… I guess what I'm most happy about is that everyone had a good time. And everyone benefited from their time in Colorado.

Interestingly enough, Carly and Laura were not feeling very good after the day back in competition. They felt horrible from the stress. They were saying how nice it was to have been at the ranch and to have de-stressed. I hadn't actually felt like there was a lot of stress in the hotel and at the COMMplex since I'd been living it. But, being out, they said that the stress hit them like a ton of bricks when they came back. Wow — I guess when you're in a situation, your body just adjusts, or you collapse.

One thing I was really looking forward to when this thing was over was resting my eyes. There were so sore from the altitude, the sun, and the bright set lights. They had been bloodshot since the first day and I'm sure I looked (to the folks watching) like I was smoking drugs on set every day. Which I was not, by the way.

{ RICH SCHEFREN }
DAY 11 AND

L ast day of competition!

I still had to make it past the Day 11 round, but, wow, it was the last day!

Since Joel had been cranky and Charles had been sick, we still had to finish up the Execution Challenge. This time it was only the team leaders who were brought up on stage to face the judges.

Charles was feeling much better (which was good).

We had to explain what we'd done with the ticket "sales" and why we'd done it. Let me tell you, if I wasn't already good at: 1) defending myself and, 2) being ready to explain myself, I was getting mighty good at it.

I don't think the judges were very impressed with what any of the teams did to guerrilla market their tickets. It was too bad that they didn't give us any examples of what we could have done. Sometimes, NIM producers, **constructive criticism** is a very good thing. How are we supposed to learn? Suggestions! Suggestions! Suggestions!

Anyway, Nico came through for me — his tickets having generated the most attendees. We won the challenge! And he and I won Joel's Adsense DVD set.

Thor and Charles had to go into the Judgement Room.

Thor was eliminated. I don't know why it was him and not Charles. I don't remember hearing a reason. Maybe, at this point in the game, Joel didn't really need a reason. It might just be who he saw a JV with and who he didn't. And that's all there is to it.

After we were paired down to two, all my stress seemed to just disappear. Maybe it was the essential oil that Kimberly gave me (I had used some that morning on my wrists.) I don't know. But I didn't have stress anymore. Maybe I was just totally and completely overtired to the point of absolute exhaustion? I don't know.

All I know is that I had been nervous for every challenge but this day's.

Rich Schefren was our Classroom teacher. I already spoke about him in the opening chapter when Charles and I were in the Judgement Room. Rich is the coach to the Internet marketing gurus.

He talked to us about business building.

It was a pretty empty Classroom — hollow with only me and Charles there to listen.

Rich said you need:

» Environment

» Business

» Marketing

» You

... to win in business. And you need those four things to all interact together.

If you can capture someone's attention, you can get rich. But it's very hard to get the attention of overloaded consumers.

Is there a way to get their attention and keep it?

The easiest thing to get your consumer to do is "action." Maybe you can get them to open an email or go to a website. "Desire" is the next step up the ladder. Can you get them to desire your product? Can you keep their "interest?" People have short attention spans. Yes you got them to action, then desire, but are they interested? And finally, if you can pique their interest and keep them reading and doing… you have their "attention." And that's the hardest thing to get.

And, remember, you're only as good as your reputation. So make sure you get a good reputation… and keep it.

The definition of marketing is, really, bringing the market to desire your product or service.

Perception is reality these days. You need to figure out how you want to be positioned because you'll be positioned whether you like it or not.

Position yourself as an expert. When you specialize in something, you're perceived as the expert.

You really need to understand your audience if you're going to sell to them. This is a common theme throughout the Internet Marketers' talks. Write for your audience. Choose titles for them. Think like them… but make sure to be different than your competition. You don't want to say the same thing as everybody else.

LIFE LESSON 18: Wherever you can… be different.

Different in business is not like different in high school. In high school, kids try to be different just to be different — to make a statement. The kids in my high school who tried to be different from the popular clique found themselves unpopular because they weren't accepted.

But business is different. Think about your customers, or your potential customers. Why would they buy from you if they can already buy the same thing from somebody established? Would you buy from you? Remember… they don't know you or how great you are. So think about how you can offer them something different, something special, and lure them away from your competition.

Find your unique talent and tell the world about it.

Make tough decisions about marketing opportunities. That's huge. There are so many techniques out there. And I'm sure that lots of them are good. But you only have so many hours in the day. Do one or two… leave the rest alone.

LIFE LESSON 19: Pick one or two things – and see them through.

My dad is a very good consumer. Like most people, he loves the idea of the quick-fix. I already mentioned that he is getting into building websites. I am so proud of him. He's a man in his mid-50s and he knows nothing about the world of HTML or Java. He's learning by going to seminars and listening to gurus. But he's buying their products. And buying. And buying.

Almost everybody has him on their lists and he gets bombarded with daily emails trying to get him to buy. I think he's bought about five or six DVD sets or coaching club memberships that are supposed to tell him how to build a website from conception to completion… but he hasn't built one yet because he starts, gets frustrated, and then gets wowed by another product and goes in that direction.

He will never get to where he wants to go unless he focuses his attention (thanks Mark Joyner) and puts his energy into finishing what he wants to do.

Anyway, back to Rich's talk…

Rich says "you don't want to be considered the best — you want to be considered the ONLY one who can solve the problem." That's your goal.

Get an original idea. An idea, really, is:

Right Target Market

+

Right Offer

+

Right Marketing

Get all of those together, and you'll shine.

There are **four required elements of an irresistible offer**:

1   It solves an urgent, pressing problem

2   It does so with a solution that is uniquely superior

3   That solution is backed up by as much proof as possible

4   It has an appealing proposition that is hard to resist

There are **three levels of proof**:

1   Proof that you've done it

2   Proof that you've helped others

3   Proof that you can help a true moron

Use number one only if you show how your problem was so much worse than theirs could ever be. You don't want people saying "Yeah, well, she did it, but she's so smart, blah, blah, blah."

Really what you want to do is show that you can and have helped a true moron. People don't want to feel stupid. So if you've helped someone who is obviously way more stupid (or worse off) than they are — that's proof that you can help them.

But don't try to use a lot of hype when you sell. People can see through that and it reduces your believability. You'll sell less. So use more verbs than adjectives in your copy.

How can you eliminate your customers' risk?

» Always incorporate future benefit into the guarantee

» Be dramatic in your explanation… "If your vision doesn't return to 20/20, I want you to take a hammer and smash the glasses to one million pieces and then send those pieces back for a full refund."

Proof and scarcity make your customers accept claims and encourage them to act quickly. You want to get the reputation for scarcity.

Here's an interesting bit of information: **the more you give away, the more people will want to buy from you.** Weird, I know — but true.

This is also true: **the sooner you ask for money, the less you'll get.**

Basically, really focus on building the trust and respect of your clients and you will be paid.

Here's another business tip… come up with your own terms for things. Don't use other people's. You want to get ownership and authority. Plus, when you make up terms and they're Googled, guess whose site is going to come up first? Yup.

You really need to engage your market. It's not enough to just interrupt or inform. Remember, this is an era of total competition. You need your customers — they don't need you. They're not looking for you. Just be consistent with your promises and deliveries — and you will be welcome.

If you want to win in the Attention Age, you have to ask yourself two things:

>> What do you know about your customers and market that your competition does not?

>> Do your marketing activities benefit your customers?

It all boils down to "how well do you really know yourself?"

Take your strengths and figure out how to create value from them. You should try to do what you do best — every day. Think about what problems you are uniquely capable of solving.

Think about this… great talkers rule. Talkers have always ruled. They will continue to rule. The smart thing is to join them.

Learn how you come across to people.

That is a very interesting subject. I know that the way I think I come off is not the way others see me. I think that I'm fun, outgoing, a bit shy, courageous, competitive, always willing to try new things, fairly liberal and witty. But when people first meet me, they think I'm quiet, shy, honest, conservative, and snobby.

I was shocked when I first found this out. I'm not that way at all. In fact, I hate when people describe me as quiet and shy. I'm not quiet, I'm just selective about who I talk to and what I say. But, to them, I realized, that comes off as quiet and shy.

Now, after people get to know me, then they see the "real" me… if I let them. Most people at my JOB have no idea of the real me. But why would they? I don't let them.

There was this girl at my high school. We called her the "pretty bitch." She was a grade ahead of me and my friends and she never talked to us. She acted like she was the queen of the world (and she was quite pretty.) Anyway, we thought she was really stuck up (and we should have known, we were pretty stuck up ourselves.) Later, I worked with her, and I discovered that she was really a very nice girl. She was just very shy. In fact, she didn't really have a lot of friends. She hung around with her younger sister a lot. Interesting, huh?

Never be afraid. What's more important than talent? Guts. You can't be afraid to fail.

You have to have a plan. To do a JV with Joel Comm (or anybody, really), we had to ask ourselves a number of questions:

» What do I bring to the table?

» How can I align it with where Joel is at?

» How will his reputation improve?

» How will my marketing alone improve the lives of my prospects?

» How do I plan on engaging my market?

» How do I want to be positioned and how will I achieve that?

Our marketing plan:

1 Define my goals

2 Define my market

3 Define my strategy

4 Define my tactics — the specifics

The most important part of a new business is getting money in — so focus your energy strategically.

With Rich done speaking, it was time for the final Execution Challenge of the competition. This was it.

We would have four hours to create a JV proposal plan for Joel. This would be a real business plan — one that would be used should we be chosen to be the Next Internet Millionaire.

There would be an actual product launch — in November of this year.

Basically, we needed to come up with a product and completely describe the plan and how the product will become a success. We would have up to 20 minutes to present it.

I really didn't have product ideas. I have many interests, but how they related to Joel Comm and his list of people was beyond me. It was very interesting to work through the process of identifying my talents and what Joel might be looking for. I knew what I could bring to the table — what my strengths were. So, the judges and I brainstormed to come up with a product.

{ SECTION 5 }

NEXT STEPS

234

{ AFTER-THOUGHTS }

After the presentations, Charles and I went into the Judgement Room — and that's where you met us at the beginning of this book.

You know that we both won the opportunity to do a JV with Joel Comm.

Like I said, I highly doubt that it was planned. But I will never know. What I can say is that you never know about people until you've worked with them. I'm sure that Joel had some ideas going into this competition, but I don't know what they were or if they changed. And I'm sure I never will.

I can say that I'm very grateful to have had the opportunity to learn from Joel, the gurus, and the other very amazing contestants.

Charles and I pretty much came out of the Judgement Room and into the NIM Wrap Party. The other contestants were so happy for us, albeit a bit envious. Some definitely weren't as chatty as others, which is weird because I know that if I had lost, those people would have been way friendlier. I guess that's just the way some people are. And some were quite drunk already, having started on the gin a bit earlier.

Joel came up to me and gave me his business card, telling me "You're going to need this." It was all so surreal. The whole experience, really. I was in total and complete shock after winning.

I got a lot of pictures with all of the contestants and crew. And we got to sit in on the presentation for all of the crew who worked so hard behind the scenes to get the show up and running. Way to go guys!

I wrote the following in my journal the night I won. I was a bit drunk at the time, having celebrated quite thoroughly all night with friends until they left (so bear with me).

I'm so happy. I'm so ecstatic. I wish I could tell... but I can't. I have to make everybody wait.

I can't believe I won. I can't believe I won. I can't believe I won!

I could just cry... but I won't. I'm alone in a hotel room. Drunk and wrapped in a towel. That would be sad and weird.

It's 4:30 a.m. and I have to leave for the airport in two hours.

I have to pack first. It's not at all done... The gold shirt never showed up. Sucks.
(This is in reference to my shirt that mysteriously went missing from my hotel room)

I can't believe all the work that has to be done, but I'm so excited.

I can't believe I'm the next Internet millionaire.

"So thank you for voting me now I'm the next Internet millionaire. Yes thank you for voting me, it's great to be the next Internet mill-ionnn-aire!"

End of NIM... back to reality.

236

And, as a tribute to Eminem, "oops there goes gravity." Funny how I keep quoting Eminem. I don't even listen to his music, only that one song. But it's so relevant

As for the writing, excuse its simplicity. Did I mention the booze and extreme lack of sleep? I just wanted you to get a feel for my excitement.

{ I'M QUITTING }
—YOUR LOSS

I'll be honest with you — it took me three weeks to the day of getting back to my government job to hand in my notice.

When I said I was scared, I wasn't kidding.

I had won. Won the opportunity to JV with Joel Comm — and I was nervous about my future.

I didn't even want to stay in government. I hated it — the confinement. The government box

But I was scared.

I made every excuse in the book.

First, there were three women in total on our web team. One had just left to go on secondment for a year, the other was going on vacation until the end of August. Well, how could I leave my boss when I was the only web person left? I couldn't do that to her. Legally, I only owed her two weeks. Yes, she would have hated me and would have never given me a good reference. But would I have needed her reference? Not bloody likely.

But I still felt like I owed it to her to be there when she needed me. Even though she hadn't made me a permanent employee or anything, I did feel like she did her best to give me jobs and develop the department using my strengths. This is not a very government thing to do and, therefore, is rare. So I didn't want to leave her in the lurch.

239

Good enough. But I also didn't put in my resignation when the two-weeks-until-the-end-of-August date passed. Why this time? Well, I told myself that I was doing a really great job of managing the "working both at home and at the office," so maybe I should just "wait and see."

Finally, I decided that enough was enough. I wasn't accomplishing as much as I had wanted to at home and I was really starting to not care about my day job. In the meantime, I found that I was getting sucked back into projects that would likely cause me to have to stay late or work weekends. That wouldn't help my personal business at all. I mean, there is a limit to how much a person can do — and I couldn't do both.

Think about it. You work a minimum of seven hours a day, plus lunch. That's eight hours. Then you have to get up and get ready. That's another half an hour (if you're quick like me.) Then you have to get to and from work. And change when you get home. That's a total of 10 hours out of your day.

But that doesn't mean that you have 14 hours left to work. You have to sleep for eight. So automatically, that leaves you with six. But, in that six, you have to make supper, clean up, grocery shop, do laundry, iron your clothes, have some down-time (or you'll collapse), shower, go to the gym, run errands, see friends, etc.

That only leaves a couple of hours per night max to work on your personal business. In the few weeks that I tried to do both, I found that I could work all weekend, then I did okay on Monday and Tuesday. But Wednesday through Friday, I was beat. I had absolutely no creativity left. No desire to learn. My body needed a break. I was staying up until four or five in the morning, going to the JOB the next day…

And I had started drinking two lattes per day!

Not good.

Anyway, I eventually realized that really, I was just scared. And that made me mad. So I knew what to do. I wrote up my notice and gave three weeks to my boss.

And you know what... it felt damn good.

> ## LIFE LESSON 20: When you jump out of your comfort zone and it feels good — you know it's right.

It's still a little scary. I admit it. But, it's not the end of the line. If I fail, and can't support myself, I have confidence enough in my abilities that I can go out and get another job. I can consult. I can work on a project by project basis. I can maybe even call up some of these guys I met and ask (beg) for work.

I have options.

But can I say again?...

IT FEELS SO GOOD TO LEAVE THE JOB THAT I KNEW I DIDN'T BELONG IN.

After she got over the shock of my letter, my boss told me she wished me luck, that she was a little envious, and that "it was very difficult to try and fit me into a government box." And, you know what? I think that was the best compliment she ever gave me.

WHAT DO
{ YOU LOVE? }

I know what you're thinking… you're thinking "Well, that's all well and good, Jaime. Thanks for the info. But I don't know what I want to do."

Well, guess what? I had no idea either. If it makes you feel better, I still don't know. Oh, don't worry. I have some ideas. And I'm getting more and more. And I will keep getting more and more, the more I learn.

But I did figure out how to narrow down what my interests are and what I like to do. And when you figure that out, you can easily connect the dots to what would make you happy in a career.

The best way to find a career that you're passionate about is to ask yourself a few questions. These might seem like easy questions, but be warned, you need to think about them. You want be thorough or you won't get the answers you're looking for.

1 When I was a kid, what did I love to do?

2 What things interest me? (i.e. What books do I own? What magazines do I get? And write down the items you really enjoy, not the stuff you pick up for show.)

3 If I could do any job I wanted, what would it be? (don't be practical with this question)

4 If I could work anywhere in the world, what place would I choose?

5 I felt the best and most powerful when I was doing?

6 I never, ever, want to do this/these again, ever.

7 What do others think my skills are?

Make out long lists. Then analyze. You'll find the results very interesting. I did.

I won't get very deep into this, but I'll tell you a little bit about my process.

When I was a little kid, I loved being...

» On camera (my parents bought one when I was one less than one month old)

» Creative (I had a band with my brother, I constantly redesigned my bedroom, I played very intricate games with My Little Ponies)

» In charge (I hated rules. Being the oldest, I loved making up the rules and organizing the events)

» Dancing (I took tap, jazz, ballet and baton from the age of four to fifteen)

» Organizing huge events (I organized my parents' 25th wedding anniversary party — huge event with out-of-town guests)

» Writing (I've written five screenplays and a novel)

What else interests me?

» Reading fiction, but haven't had any time for it in the past year or so

» *InStyle* Magazine — my guilty pleasure

» Movies

» Languages (I speak English, French and some, but very little, Spanish)

If I could do any job, I'd...

» Produce movies that I wrote, and act in them. They would have a decently high, but not atrociously high, budget, and an A-list cast. They would make money since they wouldn't cost a lot. And they would be shown in movie theatres and have a place on a Blockbuster shelf.

If I could work anywhere...

» I don't like to be locked down to locations. I love traveling and experiencing different places. My ideal job would be something where I could pick up and move whenever and wherever I wanted to. Just to try out new places.

I felt that I was at my best when I was...

» Confident in my abilities

» Challenged

» Interested in what I was doing

» Constantly doing something different or when I had to be super-focused for a short period of time

» In charge of or working with a group of people I respected and who respected me back

» In the limelight

» Having fun

I never want to _____ ever again.

» Work with incompetent people

» Work with people who don't care about their jobs

» Work set hours like 9 to 5 or 8 to 4

» Work in a cubicle

» Ask for time off and depend on a "yes" from someone else to plan my life

» Work for a set salary

» Commute during rush hour traffic (subway trains are jam-packed like sardines)

Others think I am good at…

» Brainstorming

» Creating

» Speaking in public or at meetings

» Learning new things

» Being strategic and analytical

» Exciting a group

» Leading a team

Anyway, I'm not trying to go on and on about myself. These are just quick thoughts about how I answered these questions. You need to go deeper to find out your answers. I did. I had pages of answers.

When I asked myself those questions and actually did the exercise, the answers were obvious. I just wasn't looking for them. The questions made me look and re-focus, and now I'm setting up a career that these answers pointed me to. So many things I found interesting and fun are going to be incorporated into my websites. I'm going to write. I'm going to be in movies. I'm going to design. And I'm going to put up different websites according to my interests. I can do everything.

And so can you.

Just a quick note. Before you get too involved — you might want to go to a domain purchasing site and buy your name.

Right after I was announced as a finalist for *The Next Internet Millionaire* — some bottom-feeding jerk went out and bought www.jaimeluchuck.com. People do this, and they are called Squatters. Unfortunately, even though it's apparently illegal, you can't really do anything about it.

I had to buy my name back. Thankfully, Joel talked to him and he basically gave it back to me. I was lucky. Someone else bought www.jamieluchuck.com (my name spelled incorrectly — I'm not sure if he even knows he did that). He wants $5,000 — good luck buddy.

Remember everyone, my name is **Jaime** (spelled like J'aime — "I love" in French) **not Jamie** (the masculine spelling and more like Jam-ie). I'm named after Jaime Summers, the Bionic Woman (although I've never seen the show, she sounds cool).

Anyway, domain names are cheap. They're, like, $6.95 per year. And I would highly recommend going out and buying yours if you think you might ever want it. You never know. I didn't think ahead because I didn't know what I wanted to do. And then it was too late. Some creep went and stole it… and there are no other Jaime Luchucks so it wasn't like it was some dude who happens to have the same name as me.

247

{ COLD TURKEY }
OR A SLOWER ROAST

I quit my job cold turkey — that's how I like to do things. Whenever I make a decision, I have to do it or it drives me crazy. Sometimes I think that quality of mine drives the people around me crazy. But I did it — bam! All or nothing.

But I have no dependants other than a trusty ginger-colored cat named Kahlua.

For some people, although it might feel nice to just quit, it might not be a smart decision to walk up to your boss and hand in your notice.

If you have others to think about or you don't want to crawl into debt before you make money... that doesn't mean that you're out of luck. There are ways to wean yourself off your job as you work to be on your own or do whatever you want to do.

First, do Mark Joyner's Simple.ology... PLEASE!!

It's very strategic. Even if you don't use the software, write it down on a piece of paper — step by step what you have to do in order to get off the ground. This way you know and you can cross off. I work best being able to cross off.

And little steps are better than big ones. That way you have something to cross off all the time... and you won't miss anything.

Next, look at your work schedule and what you can afford, or what your job will afford you, to do. Can you live earning less money? Will your job allow you to work less time?

Here's the thing...

Some jobs will allow you to mix up your schedule.

» Flex time: you can move around your work hours (work 7:00 to 3:00 instead of 9:00 to 5:00 so you can have more time in the evenings)

» Split shifts: a lot of waiters do this; it's morning and evening shifts with the afternoons off (if you work best in the afternoon or have a lot of business set-up appointments to make, this could be good for you)

» Telecommuting: work from home (this way you avoid travel time and can get some household chores done on breaks)

» Part time: you work less hours for less pay

If your job won't allow a different schedule, you could look at alternatives, but still safe methods, of making money.

» Temp work: join an agency that will place you in a position based on your skills and what the company is looking for (you can join specialty agencies to fit your skillsets, and ultimately make more money)

» Freelancing: contract your own work (this is only a good option if this is the way you ultimately want to go. Freelancing is not easy and it takes a while to build up your business)

If you can afford it, working part-time jobs like being a waitress can bring in a lot of extra money... much more than a typical part-time job. When I waited tables, I would bring in at least $70 in tips per shift (and that was at a low-paying restaurant). I think my highest shift was over $700 (granted, that was New Year's Eve).

There are a lot of websites where you can find small jobs. If you're a designer or programmer, websites like sitepoint.com or elance.com offer jobs. You just have to be willing to grab things and do them on short notice.

What you have to remember is that it's very easy to get used to the lifestyle your job affords. Mine affords me a great one-bedroom apartment in downtown Toronto. I can go out whenever I want. I buy clothes and shoes. I don't watch my money when I grocery shop (if I ever get around to it.) It's nice.

Going out on my own means that I'm going to have to start watching. I'm going to have to pay attention to what I'm spending and on what... for now anyway. Ultimately, I know I will be in a better position, but you have to be prepared to sacrifice today to get tomorrow. If you're not prepared to do that... don't quit your day job.

Despite what I said earlier, you can make small advancements in your personal career while working at your business. I have written many screenplays and a novel while working for the government. I was actually going to call my film company Govonca as a joke because I did so much work on it in the downtime of my job (govonca is government of Ontario, Canada). I also worked on the weekends. I opened a film company and we shot a short film. I worked as an actress on a number of productions. And I shot both of my audition videos for NIM while I was working full time.

So it can be done... it's just not fun.

You have to be really careful to keep yourself healthy. Eat well and make sure you get some time off — or you'll burn out. And quickly. It's weird... the more you want something, the harder you work. But then, the quicker you burn out. So that's my warning.

I should mention two very large pitfalls of working on your own (if that's what you're thinking of doing.).

If you leave a job to go into business for yourself — beware two things:

» Procrastination

» Solitary confinement

When you work for yourself — nobody is there to tell you what to do. If you sleep in until noon every day, nobody's going to write you up or call you into the office for a *little chat*. You can watch a movie, talk on the phone, IM with friends, email old co-workers (hey — they've got time on their hands.) You can do whatever you want. But while your co-workers are just pissing away time until it's 5:00, you are wasting work time. Time is money. And you'll never get it back.

If you want a four-hour workday, you'll never get it by procrastinating.

I am very bad at procrastinating — which is to say that I'm very good at it. I wrote this book many a night until past 4:00 a.m. and then left for work at 8:30. And that's not because I was work-ing non-stop from the time I got home from work. It was because I didn't start until 10:00 or 11:00 p.m.

I'm an extrovert. I enjoy the company of people. Working by yourself on the Internet at home is not social. There are no people around to talk to. That is dangerous. Again, since I am new to this… I don't have any answers yet. I'm just warning.

Right now, I have a lot of people I can call up. I know a lot of teachers who have the summer off. But that is almost over. Luckily, both my dad and brother run their own companies and we are planning a regular check-in thing… but we have to be very careful because the Luchucks are very good at spending hours on the phone. And what did I say earlier? Yes… time is money. I'm also planning on meeting my old co-workers for lunches…and hopefully making some new friends in my business in Toronto.

A few other bad-business tips to avoid:

» Non-stop cell phone or BlackBerry use

» Always talking about your business

» Never leaving the house

» Living in pajamas

» Excusing extreme start-up debt

NEXT INTERNET
{ MILLIONAIRE }

Now, just so you know — I'm not yet officially a millionaire. I'm just getting started on my path. I learned from some very impressive and successful people, gurus, contestants and producers. And I've had the opportunity to make some amazing connections.

And I'm living my dream.

I didn't want to work for somebody else. And I'm not. I work for me — doing what I want to do. It might not have been what I always planned to do, but it contains elements of all my interests. And I can morph what I'm doing the more successful I get.

You can too.

Just because I was on *The Next Internet Millionaire* doesn't mean that I have an advantage in achieving success over you or anybody else.

Yes, I learned from exciting people. But I took amazing notes and transcribed them all in this book so you have them.

Yes, I now have contacts. But you only need one or two friends in the business. I'm not friends with everybody who was in the show — and we're not even in the same city.

Yes, I get to use Joel Comm's list for my first venture. But you can buy lists and make lists.

I've given you all of the knowledge I learned at NIM. You have the same advantages as me.

255

In the competition, as in life, we didn't get a lot of constructive criticism. And in case you didn't notice, my team lost a lot. All I can tell you is just never give up hope. Keep trying. Keep analyzing. Keep smiling. And keep on going.

Keep believing in yourself. Know that you can and will do it. Don't doubt it for a second. Because if you don't believe in yourself... no one else will (unless you're really lucky and have amazing people surrounding you like I do.)

This might sound really cheesy... but I want you to be the next Internet millionaire.

So do it...

"And... Action!"

{The End}

Y ou read the book. You're ready to start. You want to live your dream…

Go to **www.InternetMillionaireWorkbook.com** and

DOWNLOAD YOUR
FREE INTERNET MILLIONAIRE
WORKBOOK
and get fast-tracked to success!

The workbook is an excellent way to review the steps to success listed in this book. It's the perfect way to get you thinking about how these steps can work with your business ideas and your life.

The free downloadable Internet Millionaire Workbook is the perfect supplement to From Cubicle Slave to the Next Internet Millionaire (CSNIM).

Among its many major benefits, the workbook:

» Revisits crucial points from CSNIM

» Guides you on how to practically apply knowledge found in the book

» Asks important thought-provoking questions about each and every step to success

» Sets specific action points

» Gets you thinking and working towards your ultimate goals

If you want to get out of your cubicle job and start living your dream in as little time as possible — you won't want to miss this.

Site URLs change occasionally, so please send me an email at info@jaimeluchuck.com if you encounter a broken link.

{ SECTION 6 }

APPENDIX

APPENDIX A: PRODUCT

{ INFORMATION }

Please check out www.JaimeLuchuck.com for updated versions of and up-to-date links to product information found in this book.

APPENDIX B: NOTE TO
{ NIM CAST }

C ast members of Season 1 of *The Next Internet Millionaire*:

» Debbie Ducic

» Carly Taylor

» Steve Schuitt

» Jason Henderson

» Christine Schaap

» Laura Martin

» Nico Pisani

» Alisande Chan

» Jason Marshall

» Thor Schrock

» Charles Trippy

» Jaime Luchuck

NOTE TO CAST MEMBERS...

The book was not written in order to dish dirt on you guys or any of our private moments off camera. Although I did journal my experiences in Colorado, I excluded many details that I found to be personal moments, criticisms or arguments/dislikes between cast members.

I felt that I only included, for the most part, comments and happenings that either looked favorably on all of us, or that would have been caught on camera anyway.

Nothing that I said was in malice, and if anyone was hurt by what is in this book, I sincerely apologize.

I believe that the cast of NIM is a group of amazing people who I know will do many great things.

Even though the show has publicized that I may not have gotten along with everyone, that doesn't mean that I don't respect what they have done in business, nor does it mean that they are bad people.

The *Next Internet Millionaire* was a game… and anyone watching should realize that you are being shown what the producers and editors are allowing you to see. They're looking for the drama…don't crucify members of the cast. Just sit back and enjoy.

{ ABOUT THE AUTHOR }

Jaime Luchuck (that's **Jaime, not Jamie**) is a writer, actor, web designer and communications consultant. She now adds full-time entrepreneur to her list of credits.

Having recently appeared on the world's first Internet reality show, *The Next Internet Millionaire* (*"The Apprentice"* meets You Tube), Jaime learned the skills necessary to quit her day job and start her own business.

Her website www.JaimeLuchuck.com is her business card. Check it out to see what she's up to and get the most up-to-date information. Knowing her creative style and Starbucks-fueled energy... both her site and her business are sure to keep morphing and growing.

Jaime currently lives in downtown Toronto, but travels whenever she can.

9 781600 373725